G000244029

kittens
are
EVIL

Little Heresies in Public Policy

Charlotte Pell

Rob Wilson

Toby Lowe

Published by:
Triarchy Press
Station Offices
Axminster
Devon
EX13 5PF
United Kingdom

+44 (0)1297 631456
info@triarchypress.net
www.triarchypress.net

© Triarchy Press, 2016

All rights reserved.

No part of this publication may be reproduced, stored in a retrieval system
or transmitted in any form or by any means including photocopying,
electronic, mechanical, recording or otherwise, without the prior written
permission of the publisher.

A catalogue record for this book is available from the British Library.

Print ISBN: 978–1–911193-08-1

Epub ISBN: 978-1-911193-09-8

Cover artwork by James Castleden, www.jamescastleden.com

Contents

Contents

Acknowledgements

The editors would like to acknowledge the Centre of Knowledge Innovation Technology and Enterprise (KITE) and the Business School at Newcastle University for its support of the Little Heresies seminar series, from which the chapters in this book are drawn.

The book is named after the first seminar, 'Kittens are Evil' delivered by Dr Toby Lowe on the problem with Outcome Based Accountability. The publication of this book is part of KITE's wider commitment to being part of the ongoing debate in local, national and international communities working to develop new ways of thinking about the future of public services and ways to innovate our relationships in order to build a positive future. Most importantly we would like to acknowledge the brilliant speakers and engaged audiences who have made the series such a success. Without them none of this would have been possible.

To keep up to date with upcoming Little Heresies please follow: @KiteResearch on Twitter or see the KITE website: www.ncl.ac.uk/kite

Professor Rob Wilson,
Director of KITE, Business School, Newcastle University

Dr Toby Lowe,
Senior Research Associate, KITE, Business School, Newcastle University

Charlotte Pell,
Visiting Fellow, KITE, Business School, Newcastle University

Foreword

Saying that 'payment by results' is fundamentally flawed is like saying kittens are evil. It's heresy.

The official consensus around payment by results is that it's a no-brainer, and if there are problems with it in practice, it's your fault: you're not doing it right. Coercive and simplistic thinking informs a whole range of practices aimed at improving public services, so good people try hard to make bad initiatives, based on bad theory, work. Teething troubles, poor governance, bad apples and unintended consequences are cited as reasons for high-profile failures, such as disability assessments, Universal Credit and the Troubled Families initiative.

This book argues that best efforts and poor excuses aren't good enough. The authors describe how a bad system beats well-meaning individuals every time. They argue that no amount of tinkering, re-branding or good governance can compensate for the serious and widespread harm inflicted by a fundamentally flawed set of beliefs. George Monbiot succinctly described these beliefs and their consequences in *The Guardian* (April 2016):

> *We respond to these crises as if they emerge in isolation, apparently unaware that they have all been either catalysed or exacerbated by the same coherent philosophy; a philosophy that has – or had – a name. What greater power can there be than to operate namelessly?*

So pervasive has neoliberalism become that we seldom even recognise it as an ideology. We appear to accept the proposition that this utopian, millenarian faith describes a neutral force; a kind of biological law, like Darwin's theory of evolution.

The authors of this book challenge manifestations of neoliberal assumptions in public services – through family intervention, personalisation, numerical targets, marketisation, league tables, economies of scale, inspection and payment by results.

At the heart of neoliberalism is a belief about people. Individuals are perfectible: anyone can (and should) be successful, to 'make something of themselves', if they only try hard enough. If they are unsuccessful, they should be forced to compete harder. (Try watching Ken Loach's *I, Daniel Blake*.) If only we ate less, exercised more, stopped getting older, were more enterprising, ticked the right boxes, remembered our unique customer reference number, were digital by default and frankly were more service-shaped. Wouldn't that make the government's job easier?

A systems view has a very different starting point. This book argues that it is the system itself that is troubled, not families or individuals. As in finance, neoliberal 'quick wins' all too often turn into long-term disaster, and it is the same in the public sector that has internalised its thinking.

The system is where we need to intervene. Attending to systems and their consequences for people is the only sustainable route to better lives and a better society.

This book isn't a conscious attempt to design a new system, although in places it makes a start. It does, however, provide strong evidence for public sector professionals, academics and policy makers to see neoliberalism for what it is – not a neutral or inevitable force, but a set of intentional and man-made political beliefs. By seeing it, we can help politicians who believe in something different, to create a new orthodoxy.

Charlotte Pell,
Visiting Fellow, KITE, Business School, Newcastle University

Simon Caulkin,
Writer and editor

Editorial

This is an unconventional book for unconventional times. In 2012, when we started 'Kittens are Evil' and the subsequent Little Heresies journey, the world we saw looked quite different albeit in subtle ways. For example, the rhetoric around the improvement and modernisation of public services was and continues to be stuck in the groove of the supposed superiority of the private sector, yet a vast range of public services have been run by the private and third sector for over thirty years. This is no longer an experiment; New Public Management, also known by its shorthand of NPM (broadly neo-liberal thinking and practice applied to the public sector) is the dominant paradigm. In the past five years its application has intensified, especially in England, where all aspects of public and community life now seem open to the application of what Ferlie *et al* (1996) termed the 3Ms – Markets, Management and Measurement.

Our aim is not just to show that importing management thinking wholesale from the private sector creates perverse incentives for public sector organisations and those who work for them, because that is already well documented by academics and other commentators (some of whose views appear here). Such debates about NPM are also in the public domain, particularly as parts of the media, usually unsympathetic to public services, have begun to routinely report the abuses. What is more important to consider is the damage NPM does to the way we as a society think and talk about public services, returning to the sorts of framing of debates that we had at the beginning of the twentieth century, including the morality of the language used such as 'the deserving and underserving poor'.

As the state shrinks ever farther and more rapidly from some areas, in ways that only a decade ago would have been regarded as unthinkable, the need to challenge the prevailing orthodoxy has become even more important. The point of the heresy series was and is to provide a public platform for challenging current assumptions through talks based on analysis in specific contexts. The Heretics we have selected for this book challenge the effect of NPM on their specialist fields of interest or practice, and offer an alternative way of thinking about and/or doing the work.

With regards to the tools of Performance Management, we have dissenting contributions from Toby Lowe on 'Outcome Based' methods and Simon Guilfoyle on Targets. From Simon Duffy, John Seddon, Simon Caulkin and Kathy Evans we have trenchant accounts of the problems that government generates when politicians decide to 'fix' things, by disrupting innovation or insisting that a policy area should be marketised, and because government believes that intervention in and of itself is a good thing. The remaining two heresies are from Sue White and Stephen

Crossley who ferociously challenge the emergence of ideas which assume that we can derive policy on parenting via questionable insights from experimental research, or family policy which denies the role of government in creating the conditions in which families are struggling in the first place.

Summarising these contributions then, as well as the surprise that some of them should be heresies at all, each chapter is a challenge to what is being presented and accepted as 'taken for granted', the 'common sense'. It is the dominance of the paradigm which emphasises competition over co-operation, markets over communities, individuals over relationships, performance management over learning, national targets and league tables over local governance and, above all, the contract as the main thing that counts and informs the account.

As one of our colleagues and future heretic likes to say, operating using the principle of 'Keep It Simple Stupid' is all very well when it is simple, but 'Pretending It's Simple Stupid' is the real problem here.

Professor Rob Wilson,
Director of KITE, Business School, Newcastle University

Dr Toby Lowe,
Senior Research Associate, Business School, Newcastle University

Charlotte Pell,
Visiting Fellow, KITE, Business School, Newcastle University

Ferlie, E., Ashburner, L., Fitzgerald, L. and Pettigrew, A. (1996), *New Public Management in Action*, Oxford University Press

1. New Public Management – Dystopian interventions in public services

John Seddon

New Public Management (NPM) became a catch-all phrase for public-sector reform. It has a number of components: economy of scale, markets, targets, regulation and inspection – all thought to drive innovation and efficiency. Every UK government since Margaret Thatcher's subscribes to the belief that NPM is the right approach; no matter which party people vote for, NPM is the order of the day.

It is ironic; the phrase 'New Public Management' was coined by those who sought to argue against the reforms and the label was adopted by the protagonists. Who could argue against wanting to be 'new'?

But NPM has not delivered improvement or innovation; instead it has driven up costs and worsened services. In the 35 years of successive governments pursuing these ideas, we have doubled our expenditure on local authority services and trebled expenditure on the health service. No one would argue if there had been a two-times or three-times improvement in performance, but what is evident – everywhere you look – is public dissatisfaction with services and frequent crises.

I have invested a lot of time in studying public-sector services; the arguments here are all evidence-based. The evidence reveals that the plausible features of NPM are no more than that – plausible. Each fails to live up to its promise, but each is so plausible as to be compelling, especially for people who are entirely disconnected from the places where the work is done.

My colleagues and I have developed alternative and hugely more effective designs for public services. These designs are built on assumptions that directly contradict the NPM orthodoxy. It is the strength of the results that has enabled adoption of these methods to grow in what is a hostile, fear-driven, environment. To take the main features of NPM in turn:

Economy of scale

The idea was born in early industrial manufacturing. Bigger factories produced goods at lower unit costs. The philosophy remained unchallenged until Taiichi Ohno developed his Toyota Production System in Japan in the 1950s. Heralded as the 'Japanese Miracle', Toyota factories produced vehicles to meet consumer demand. Control of operations was in the hands of those doing the work; the worker was his own inspector – there was no independent inspection; manufacturing lines accommodated a variety of products; movement of materials worked at the heartbeat of consumer demand. The Toyota System was the first 'pull' manufacturing system – take an order, make the car. Ohno's abiding preoccupation, indeed his strategy, was to focus on reducing the time between receiving an order and receiving payment. The impact on quality was legendary and costs fell dramatically.

Ohno showed that economic performance was far better if there was a focus on 'flow' rather than 'scale'. He rejected manufacturing's obsession with unit cost, focusing instead on the whole system cost, and by managing value rather than cost, quality improved and costs fell. Few manufacturers have followed Ohno's innovation. People have been persuaded that 'lean' represents what happened in Toyota but that is a fool's conclusion (www.vanguard-method.net, animation about the failure of lean).

Services are quite different from manufacturing. In services there are no machines – the major constraint in designing and managing manufacturing activities. In services the customer is involved in production.

Economies of scale in the public sector, as promulgated by NPM, means services designed as factories. It means the separation of front and back offices, monitoring activity, specialising and standardising work, inspection, service levels and standard times. All of these things are thought to decrease costs, as they did in the early manufacturing factories. But they don't. These things cause costs to rise.

The first sign of trouble is failure demand (demand caused by a failure to do something or do something right for the customer (Seddon 2003, p26). It is an easy concept to understand and to misunderstand. People think failure demand is caused by people not doing their jobs correctly; people think failure demand can be blamed on departments. But failure demand is a systemic problem, caused by all of the system conditions that are imposed in a 'scale' design. In short, scale-designed services are both high cost and low quality services (Seddon, 2003).

Ministers compound the problems caused by industrialisation of services by sanctioning IT-led change. The litany of failing government IT projects is nothing short of astonishing, but it is something we should expect – 90% of large-scale IT programmes fail (Gauld and Goldfinch, 2006). Just one example: Iain Duncan Smith's Universal Credit (UC) will never be able to test his thesis, that paying benefits to people can be done in a way that encourages a productive life. The UC IT-dominated design will not only be likely to fail in getting built (delivery dates slip on a regular basis) but even if it gets built it will fall down on the problems described above. The rules that once governed benefits services will be transferred to an unforgiving computer. The failure to absorb the variety of demand will mean more demand into call centres (although government talks of closing them down) and, more tragically, will damage peoples' lives.

The way to design services that work is, in essence, to give customers what they need; it is to understand 'value' from the customers' point of view. This can only be done when demand, the things that customers want, is thoroughly understood. Knowledge of demand enables managers to build the expertise required to provide the right service to customers at the point of transaction. Back offices disappear, activity measurement changes from adherence to arbitrary times to measuring actual time taken. No processes are standardised as that would impede the ability to respond to the variety of customer demands. All measures in use are derived from the purpose of the service from the customers' point of view. The consequences are high-quality low-cost services (Middleton (ed), 2010., Zokaei *et al*, 2010., Pell (ed), 2012., Gibson and O'Donovan, 2014., Wilson, 2014). In a world where nothing can be done without information technology, IT development becomes the last (not the first) thing to do when developing services that work (Seddon, 2013).

Markets

Politicians believe that the free market is an essential lever for driving efficiency. Leaving aside the truth that there is no such thing as a truly free market, this has meant, in practical terms, that public services are put out to tender for the lowest prices. It has resulted in out-sourced contracts for call centres and back offices where the costs are calculated on the basis of volumes of work – yes, paying providers for handling large volumes of failure demand is an absurdity. In recent times, we have witnessed the failure of many out-sourced large-scale health and care contracts; the prices were set on the basis of historic costs with no understanding of demand and hence were bound to fail.

It is not competition that drives innovation and improvement, it is collaboration – working together for the same end.

Take, for example, services for people whose lives have fallen off the rails, whether through health and care needs, family breakdown, drugs and alcohol problems and so on. Competition has meant providers bidding for work on the basis of prices for activities. To price activities requires standardising them. The standardised offerings don't meet the variety of needs citizens have so we spend money to no avail; we don't help people get their lives back on the rails.

By contrast, involving all service providers in understanding the true nature of demand enables the development of services that are truly person-centric. Costs fall, lives are speedily put back on the rails and, most telling of all, demand falls. Happier people, stronger families and communities (Locality, 2014), shouldn't this be the purpose of public services?

Targets

Politicians believe that targets represent a quasi-market – by reporting on achievement of targets, services compete. But a target, by its nature, is an arbitrary measure. Imposing any arbitrary measure down a hierarchy distorts the system; work is organised around meeting targets, rather than citizens' needs and people 'cheat' to ensure they avoid punishment. Services meet all the targets and miss the point. Reports of 'targets met' fool politicians and commentators to believe things are working. This madness was enshrined in 'Deliverology', a word invented by Sir Michael Barber to describe what he called 'the science of delivery' during Tony Blair's government (Barber, 2007). This illusion of control through top-down targets has been spread around the globe despite its disastrous effects in the UK (Seddon, 2008: 8).

In designing an effective service we need to avoid all arbitrary measures; all measures need to be real/actual and derived from the purpose of a service from the citizens' point of view. My test of a good measure is: can it be used to both understand and improve performance?

When you study services you learn that there is a systemic relationship between purpose, measures and methods.

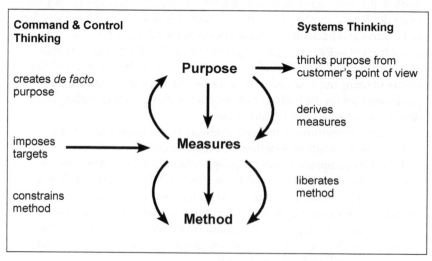

Purpose, measures, method: a systemic relationship
(Seddon, 2014:174)

Imposing arbitrary targets creates a *de facto* purpose (meet the target) and constrains method (design services around target-achievement). Deriving measures from the purpose of the service from the citizens' point of view, and using the same where the work is done, drives innovation and high morale, and motivation shifts from extrinsic (fear) to intrinsic (pride).

Politicians believe targets are the means by which we hold public services to account. True accountability requires, among other things, the freedom for public-services leaders to make choices about measures (see later).

Regulation and inspection

> *A regulation is justifiable if it offers more advantage than*
> *the economic waste that it entails.*   (Deming 1997:298)

Regulation and inspection create a regime of compliance which not only stifles innovation but drives fear into the lives of public-service managers, damaging morale. The growth of regulation has been massive, and recent. Even politicians have doubts about regulation's value – every European State has a 'better regulation' task force but things aren't getting better. The problem is that regulators also bring with them their theories of management, and that means subscribing to NPM.

Regulators go beyond targets; they frequently specify methods – how work should be designed and managed. Given their roots are in NPM, these methods are flawed or, to say the least, sub-optimal. But the deeper problem is that adherence to the regulator's ideas of methods creates a climate of compliance; success depends on it. But 'success' is no more than compliance. The economic waste associated with regulation and inspection includes the resources invested in creating specifications, the resources invested in compliance, the consequences of adherence to bad (NPM) ideas and the ubiquitous demoralisation associated with a compliance culture. Regulation is a disease.(Seddon, 2014, chapter 14).

We learned from the quality theorists many years ago that you can't improve with inspection; inspection is too late. The most egregious recent evidence is revealed in the OECD's report (OECD 2016, The Independent 29/1/16) which shows a shocking fall in standards of education – the direct result of a specifications and inspection culture. Politicians have been shown how successful the Finnish education system, which goes against the evaluation driven model, is, but they ignore the lessons as the solutions don't fit with their narrative. While we invest in a specifications and compliance industry, the Finnish system is based on the philosophy of prevention. Resources are focused on training high-quality teachers and providing them with easy-to-access support when they get to the classroom.

What has to change?

Whitehall has to change before anything else can change. To be blunt, ministers should get out of management. Think back to purpose/measures/method. It is a systemic relationship. Currently, it is dystopian in its impact.

Politicians quite rightly ought to have a view on the purposes of public services, but all choices about measures and methods have to be left to those responsible for designing and managing them – public services leaders. This would create a culture of responsibility rather than compliance.

The focus should be on transparency rather than compliance. It would mean not being able to hide behind satisfying a tick-box inspector. The 'inspection' role would shift from assessing compliance to asking what choices of methods and measures have been made and to what effect. Responsibility is the bedrock of innovation.

The scope to innovate in public services remains, but after 35 years of wrong-headed interventions we need public services leaders to be motivated to innovate. What we know from the literature on motivation is that it requires three things: Autonomy – the freedom to act, Mastery – the freedom to learn, and Purpose – a clear intent (Pink 2009). If politicians can limit their involvement to the last we stand a chance; the economic and social gains will be considerable.

Professor John Seddon is the leader of the Vanguard organisations, now working in nine countries, helping service organisations change from a conventional 'command-and-control' design to a systems design. John has received numerous academic awards for his contribution to management science and won the first Harvard Business Review/McKinsey Management Innovation Prize for 'Reinventing Leadership' in 2010.

References

Animation about the failure of Lean: www.vanguard-method.net/what-can-we-learn-from-programmes-of-change/lean/ Accessed 8/2/16

Barber, M. (2007) *Instruction to Deliver,* Politicos Publishing.

Deming, W. E. (1997) *Out of the Crisis,* MIT Press. (Seventh edition, first published 1982).

Gauld, R. and Goldfinch, S. (2006) *Dangerous Enthusiams. E-government, Computer Failure and Information System Development,* Otago University Press

Gibson, J and O'Donovan, B (2014) 'The Vanguard Method as Applied to the Design and Management of English and Welsh Children's Services Departments' *Systemic Practice and Action Research* February, Vol 27, Issue 1, pp 39-55

Ross, Eleanor. (2016) 'English teenagers 'are most illiterate in the developed world', report reveals', [Online] http://www.independent.co.uk/news/education/education-news/english-teenagers-are-the-most-illiterate-in-the-developed-world-report-reveals-a6841166.html, *The Independent*

Locality 2014, 'Saving money by doing the right thing: Why "local by default" must replace "diseconomies of scale', [Online] https://www.vanguard-method.com/v1_lib.php?current=907

OECD (2016) 'Building Skills for All: A Review of England' Authors: Małgorzata Kuczera, Simon Field and Hendrickje Catriona Windisch [Online] http://www.oecd.org/education/skills-beyond-school/building-skills-for-all-review-of-england.pdf

Pell, C. (ed.) (2012) *The Vanguard Method in the Public Sector: Case Studies Delivering Public Services that Work Vol.2'*, Triarchy Press

Pink, D. (2009) *Drive: The Surprising Truth About What Motivates Us*, Riverhead Books

Seddon, J. (2003) *Freedom from Command and Control*, Vanguard Press

Seddon, J. (2008) *Systems Thinking and the Public Sector,* Triarchy Press

Seddon, J. (2013) 'Dissolving a Dangerous Enthusiasm: Taking a Systems Approach to IT Systems', *Cutter IT Journal*, Vol. 26, April, No. 4

Seddon, J. 2014 *The Whitehall Effect: How Whitehall became the enemy of great public services and what we can do about it*, Triarchy Press

Wilson, R. (2014) 'Living the Life You Choose: The Introduction of the Vanguard Method into an Organisation Providing Support to People with Learning Disabilities', *Systemic Practice and Action Research*, February 2014, Volume 27, Issue 1, pp 57-74

Zokaei, K., Seddon, J. and O'Donovan, B. eds (2010) *Systems Thinking: From Heresy to Practice*, Palgrave Macmillan

2. Public Service Markets Aren't Working for the Public Good…or as markets

Kathy Evans

In November 1989, Kenneth Clarke, then Secretary of State for Health, published a White Paper, 'Working for patients (NHS reforms)', which proposed to introduce a split between purchasers and providers of care, GP-fundholders and a state-financed internal market, 'in order to drive service efficiency' in the National Health Service. Less than a year later, the creation of an 'internal market' in Britain's largest public service had passed into law. A new public policy idea had been born, one that discarded previous economic orthodoxy about the fundamental difference between public and private sectors within a 'mixed economy'.

This new 'public service market' idea was closely related, in terms of political ideology, to the Conservative government's parallel policy of privatising former public sector industries and functions, like telecoms and energy supply. Economically speaking, however, the 'public service market' idea was distinct from, and far more experimental than, privatisation. While privatisation simply (albeit contentiously) transferred assets and service functions from public to private sector, the 'internal market' sought to blur the very distinction between public and private sector economic activity. The government claimed that under their new policy invention (the 'internal market') the NHS would remain a public sector service: its assets would remain publicly owned; expenditure would remain taxpayer-funded; and its effective delivery would remain the democratic responsibility of elected politicians. But, they claimed, it would only become better as a public sector service by artificially simulating commercial market dynamics within its own management structures, forcing different teams and specialist units to compete with each other on the basis of their performance, creating 'customer choice' for budget-holders within the NHS, heralding the adoption of the managerial behaviours, language and disciplines associated with successful commercial businesses.

Ten years before the advent of the 'internal market' another piece of legislation had also been passed that, while separate in scope and intention at the time, would soon combine with public service market ideas to accelerate the proliferation of 'service market' orthodoxy across the public sector. The Local Government, Planning and Land Act 1980 had introduced a new duty on councils to enter into Compulsory Competitive Tendering (CCT) for all commercial works and spending they might commission, such as house-building and maintenance or highway repairs. Its stated intention was two-fold: to prevent the much-documented phenomenon of 'cronyism' and bribery in the awarding of lucrative local business contracts, and to break the 'closed shop' controls that Trades Unions were perceived to exercise over the award of contracts only to firms they approved, on worker terms and conditions that met their demands. The CCT leglislation required local authorities to put any intended contract for works and labour out to open bids, including to firms that did not meet union terms, and then required them to have a transparent record of the rationale for their decision on awarding the work, on the basis of which would provide 'best value' to the taxpayer.

At that time, the very idea of local 'public service markets' in statutory functions like elderly care or looking after abused children was unheard of. The provision of social care and community support services was itself a longstanding and often very locally idiosyncratic 'mixed economy' of public and charitable agencies, which usually had partnership agreements and grant funding arrangements that had evolved over many decades. The original compulsory tendering legislation was not overtly designed to interfere with such local arrangements between councils and charities, however the later spread of 'public service market' ideas, along with the evolution of council procurement regimes soon meant that the funding and decision-making about who should provide social care services to the public (and eventually a whole host of other statutory functions and community services) became deeply entangled with councils' interpretations of their compulsory tendering obligations.

The proliferation of competitive contracting in public services was not, however, a uniquely British phenomenon. Following the official completion of the 'single market project' in 1992, which focused on promoting 'free trade' in commercial products across all member states, the attention of the European Union shifted towards the services sector, and the development and implementation of what are now commonly referred to as the 'EU Directives'. Successive iterations of the EU's regulations for state procurement legally required open competition in the awarding of contracts (above a threshold amount) by all public bodies, and restricted the ability of governments to provide any financial 'state aid' that might give unfair market advantage to any one market competitor over others. For many professionals in the public sector today the EU directives, and their transposition into domestic procurement legislation, have become the most definitive expression of the orthodoxy that all public sector spending decisions are in essence commercial market transactions in which they, as public officials, have a duty to ensure open competition.

By 2015 the idea that almost all public functions and services are best understood and managed as open competitive markets had become such a politically orthodox view across the political spectrum that it was a consistent underpinning theme within public policy reforms during all three terms of Labour administrations between 1997-2010, and continued seamlessly in the 'Open Public Services' reforms of the Tory/LibDem coalition government of 2010-15, and to this day under the Tory administration elected in May 2015.

In practice, the extent of competitive contracting with the state for public service delivery has grown to huge proportions. In December 2014, the parliamentary Public Accounts Committee reported that, *'The private sector delivers complex services on behalf of the public sector, to the value of around £90 billion, which represents half of all public sector expenditure on goods and services.'* The voluntary services sector has also more than doubled its income from contracting with government since 2000, while public sector grant-making to charities and voluntary groups has halved. For the voluntary sector, the inexorable rise of contracting is a tell-tale sign of how far the public service market orthodoxy has spread and changed the nature of their historical partnerships with government.

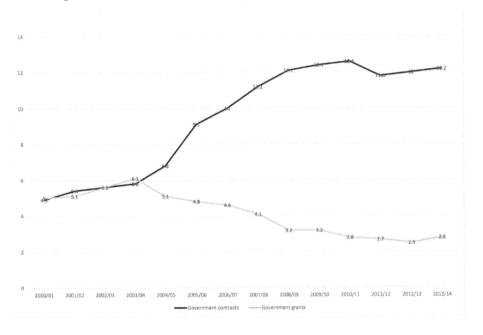

Voluntary Sector Income from Government Sources
Source: NCVO Almanac 2013
Sums on left axis are £ billions

Beneath the 'market interface' of competing for and awarding service contracts on 1-3 year cycles, the day-to-day language, design and delivery of social care practice has become profoundly shaped by commercial sales and business management disciplines – just as the architects of the 'internal market' had hoped. Service managers today, if they are to hope to 'win business', are encouraged to be able to define their product clearly; to have and to meet targets; to have data that proves their service product really 'works' (evidence of outcomes); to have done their market and competitor research; to know their unique selling point and have a perfected 'market pitch'. Successful services are deemed to be those that deliver a 'return on investment' (whether social or in terms of financial savings), which come in at a competitive price and 'unit cost'. The general modern view of 'success' for a service delivery organisation, just as it is in commercial business, is indicated by growth in turnover, which in turn delivers a market advantage through achieving economies of scale. For many public and charitable professionals today, whether working in service delivery or as commissioners and spenders of public funds, the public service market orthodoxy is so deeply embedded into their working environment they may never have experienced, or be able to imagine, a different way of organising and delivering public services.

Heresy

Public service markets do not, and cannot behave like open commercial markets. Continued reliance on open competition in the 'supply' of public services will lead to market collapse and/or new monopolies.

Well-established (but recently widely-ignored) classical economic theory already holds the key to understanding why open market competition is an inherently dysfunctional and distorted mechanism for meeting the state's public service duties. In order to see how, we have to unpick and examine some of the fundamental definitional building blocks in the public service market orthodoxy.

It takes some time to find any dictionary definition of a market that could possibly encompass public services markets. The Business Dictionary defines it thus:

> *Market (n): An actual or nominal place where forces of demand and supply operate, and where buyers and sellers interact (directly or through intermediaries) to trade goods, services or contracts or instruments, for money or barter.*

> *Markets include mechanisms or means for (1) determining price of the traded item, (2) communicating the price information, (3) facilitating deals and transactions, and (4) effecting distribution. The market for a particular item is made up of existing and potential customers who need it and have the ability and willingness to pay for it.*

The Business Dictionary definition of a market, above, could encompass the emergence of public service markets if – and only if – public spending bodies are understood to be the *existing and potential customers* generating the market's demand. While this jars with most people's understanding of who really generates the demand for public services, in fact this designation would be quite true to the original 'internal market' idea of designated, budget-holding government employees acting as customers, although common practice since then has been to term such roles as *commissioners*. In order to follow, as far as possible, this definition of a market, we will refer to the state as the 'customer' in public service market orthodoxy.

The next task is to determine what kind of market most public services markets are. It is a matter of common agreement that monopolies are 'bad markets', and 'open markets' are good, for example. But there are several other types of market too.

> "This white paper says loud and clear that it shouldn't matter if providers are from the state, private or voluntary sector – as long as they offer a great service. The old narrow, closed, state monopoly is dead."   (Cameron, 2011)

Market strucutre	No. of buyers	No. of sellers	Buyer entry barriers	Seller entry barriers	Size of firm	Product differen-tiation	Market Share	Competition
Perfect competition	Many	Many	No	No	Relatively small	No, homogene-ous product	Small	Fierce
Monopolis-tic competi-tion	Many	Many	No	No	Relatively small	Basically sub-stitutes, but not alike as brand-ing is different	Small	Fierce
Oligopoly	Many	Few	No	Yes	Average	Homogeneous differentiated	Average	High
Oligopsony	Few	Many	Yes	No	Relatively small	Homogeneous	Average	Imperfect competition
Monopoly	Many	One	No	Yes	Relatively Large	No substitute goods/services	Highest	No competition
Monopsony	One	Many	Yes	No	Relatively small	Substitute goods/services	Average	Imperfect competition

In most public service markets the state is either the largest single paying customer (e.g. schools and health, where private customers account for around 10% of all demand), or the only customer (e.g. prisons, children's homes, probation services). The table above shows that wherever the state is the dominant or sole customer (buyer) it means that public service markets are either oligopsonies or monopsonies. Many decades of development in economic market theory and learning have shown that oligopsonies and monopsonies are structurally imperfect markets, in which profound market distortions, such as price-fixing below production costs, are inherently likely, whatever the goods or services being traded. Economists have also found that if left to run their competitive course as if they were 'free' or open markets, monopsonies and oligopsonies inherently tend to result in the creation of cartels (oligopolies) and monopolies.

In other words, a monopsony customer who goes out 'to market' in order to purchase the supply of services to meet their needs (instead of meeting it themselves) will eventually end up with only one monopoly supplier left, upon whom they are completely dependent and who can then hold them hostage at over-inflated prices because they have complete command over the capacity to meet the customer's needs. In some of the longest standing areas of public service contracting there are signs that this is already happening, with a small cartel of 'too-big-to-fail' public sector contractors (e.g. G4S, Serco, Capita) evading the kind of corrective market rejection or new competitor challenge that would generally happen in an open commercial market, because the state is already too heavily reliant on their continued operations.

> ...as public service markets develop, quasi-monopoly suppliers are emerging who squeeze out competition, often from smaller companies with specific experience. Competition for government business should bring with it a constant pressure to innovate and improve. But for competition to be meaningful, there must be real consequences for contractors who fail to deliver and the realistic prospect that other companies can step in.   (Public Accounts Committee, 2014)

On a purely theoretical basis using market competition to break up 'old' state monopolies in the supply of public services will only follow a trajectory that ends inevitably in new monopolies. The alternative, and equally possible, course of events in practice will be that the inexorable (competitive) downwards pressure on price among current competing suppliers will increasingly fail to cover the actual costs of running services, and the businesses (whether private or charitable) currently running a huge volume of public services either collapse and go bankrupt, or breach and walk away from their service contracts. This will leave public bodies with major continuing statutory duties to meet for their citizens but insufficient service capacity to meet them. It is widely reported today that adult social care providers find themselves, en masse, at that brink of market collapse. Other markets, such as residential care for children, may not be far behind.

Either outcome (new monopolies or market collapse) will be catastrophic for public service users, taxpayers and for the public officials left with all the same legal duties and none of the assets, resources or expertise needed to meet them. It is essential that the orthodoxy, that greater competition will improve public services and save public money, is rejected, conclusively – for it is reliant on market competition that will in fact accelerate the worst possible outcomes for public service markets.

With business terminology and comparisons now so deeply embedded across public and charitable services, it is perhaps illustrative to look at the most basic rudimentary tenets and 'rules' in successful commercial business. If public service market proponents were right in their belief that all types and sectors of organisation are best run according to the disciplines and incentives of commercial business management, it should be the case that the keys to business success would apply equally to public service provision. But they don't.

In commercial business demand is always a good thing. Increasing the volume of customers who want to buy your product is the first and most important objective of successful business for any entrepreneur – an objective which also underpins the entire advertising and marketing industry. In public or charitable services, however, demand is not straightforwardly positive. Up to a certain point knowing that people want and appreciate the service you offer is a 'good thing'. Given the often sensitive personal and social problems that such services are there to meet, however, their need for help is nothing to celebrate or exploit, and an increasing volume of demand may be a cause for real concern, both as a service and as a society. ChildLine, for example, has reported that the numbers of children calling them to seek help for their suicidal feelings has substantially increased, year on year. As a service, the fact that they are available to respond to such distressing demand is a testament to the value of their service and the trust children have in them; the cause and implications of that rising demand, however, are clearly something about which to be deeply alarmed.

In commercial business repeat custom is brilliant. Indeed it has become prevalent to see customer loyalty reward schemes and 'product obsolescence' as strategies to promote repeat custom. In charitable and public services, if the same people are returning for your help over and over again then you need to consider the possibility that you are doing something very wrong!

In commercial business demand is your source of income. If demand is higher than you can supply you can still capitalise on it, either by raising the price (and rationing over-demand) or by investing in increased capacity to meet greater demand. The feasibility and repayment of loan finance in order to capitalise on high demand can be calculated by the projected income that will automatically be generated by being able to meet it. In public and charitable services, however, the person demanding your help does not bring with them the additional income that might help you to meet it. Whether your service is funded by taxes, donations or grants the capacity you have is finite unless or until anyone agrees to contribute more funds. A loan to invest in increased service capacity cannot easily be premised on any assumption that higher demand will generate any more income with which to repay it.

In commercial business, price is a reasonable gauge for value. When a customer decides that the price asked or negotiated for a commercial product is both affordable and reflective of its value to them, the sale can take place to the mutual satisfaction of both the customer and the seller. In general, in commercial markets, customer willingness to pay higher prices compared with others can be taken as a reasonable reflection of the relative value they place on that product. In charitable and public services the client rarely if ever pays or negotiates a price to be paid from their own pocket, and they may be inherently and completely oblivious to the costs of meeting their needs (e.g. an infant child needing expensive health care). Those who do fund the service, be they public commissioners or charitable donors, are not the consumers of it. The price of a service may, therefore, be completely unrelated to the value people place on receiving it, making 'market competition' on the basis of price comparisons an irrelevance in determining value. This disconnection between price and value can work both ways – a very expensive service could still have low satisfaction among its service users, just as a relatively low-cost, volunteer-run service may be viewed as priceless and irreplaceable by the people who rely on it.

When the fundamental tenets of good business are so different from the similarly fundamental features and dynamics of public service delivery, it should be beyond doubt that 'market forces' cannot work in the same way in both sectors either. American economist, Professor Edgar Cahn, in an open letter to the non-profit community (2007) powerfully expressed an even more fundamental reason for the incompatibility of market mechanisms with the delivery of social benefits and support. The 'core economy' to which he refers in his quote below is a term used to describe the networks of relationships within family, friendship and community, through which people support each other at no monetary charge:

> *Markets driven by monetary exchanges cannot put supply and demand together to rebuild the Core Economy because of the way that market value defines value. If quantity is scarce compared to demand, then market value is high. The opposite applies: if supply is abundant, then value goes down. We say something is dirt cheap or worthless if it is abundant.*

That definition of value devalues those very universal capacities that enabled our species to survive and evolve: our ability to care for each other, to come to each other's rescue, to learn from each other, to stand up for what's right and to oppose what is wrong. In market terms, those capacities, if abundant, are worthless. In terms of rebuilding the core economy, those values are literally price-less."

What has to change?

Our belief at Children England is that competitive service market approaches need to be suspended and replaced with collaborative action across public and charitable organisations. We worked with the TUC, Unite, Unison and a wide range of charities and council bodies, to produce a 'Declaration of Interdependence' – a charter of principles and local reforms that require no legal changes to implement, but which could radically reverse the erosion of collective resources, creativity and common cause that charities and public servants have historically shared in supporting the needs of their communities.

In imagining different ways to understand and rebuild the economics of public ownership and service, there is great inspiration to be found in the work of Elinor Ostrom, a Nobel economist who developed 'Common Pool Resourcing'. Her ideas and analysis have given shape and inspiration to a wave of examples from Europe and Scandinavia showing new ways that citizens and communities are sharing, governing and sustainably using public goods and assets such as energy, transport and public services.

It should not be overlooked, however, that the rigours and constraints of EU procurement directives are widely viewed as a barrier to any radical attempts to reject public service market orthodoxy in practice. While the UK has tended to be the most zealous interpreter of the directives, and they have become deeply embedded into our domestic law and procurement culture, the prospect of a 'Brexit' withdrawal from the European Union, and a review of all EU laws regulations in doing so, does offer an opportunity to learn from the damaging impact of approaching public services as a competitive marketplace and to construct a new and different regulatory approach to ensuring good public spending practices.

And finally, the prospect of the EU/US Transatlantic Trade and Investment Partnership, that would have entrenched the rights of companies to retain and profit from their 'market positions' in public service delivery, is something which has faded in direct relevance for the UK, with the advent of Brexit and of the election of Donald Trump, who is committed to withdraw from it. It remains the case, however, that trade negotiations and deals may still come to be viewed as vehicles through which to consolidate the idea of 'open markets' in public goods and services – and all those who care about the sustainability of public and charitable services for the people they serve should remain alert in resisting their inclusion. .

Kathy Evans, Chief Executive, Children England
@Kathy_CEO_CE

References and Further Reading

Business Dictionary, 'market' [Online] http://bit.ly/2fsbNo8

Cabinet Office, HM Government (2010) 'Open Public Service' a White Paper

Children England and TUC (July 2014) 'Declaration of Interdependence in children's services' published online only http://www.childrenengland.org.uk/wp-content/uploads/2014/07/Declaration-of-Interdependence-FINAL.pdf

Cahn, E. Prof (2007) 'It's the Core Economy, Stupid!: an open letter to the non-profit community' [onlie only] http://bit.ly/2fwbmZX

Department of Health, HM Government (November 1989) 'Working for Patients (NHS Reform): a White Paper'

Evans, K. (November 2014) 'The voluntary sector must assert its value beyond money' in "Making Good: the future for the voluntary sector" (Civil Exchange, London)

National Council for Voluntary Organisations (NCVO 2013) "Civil Society Almanac" Published by NCVO

Ostrom, Elinor; Crawford, Sue E. S. (September 1995). 'A grammar of institutions.' *American Political Science Review* (American Political Science Association via JSOR).

Ostrom, Elinor (March 1998). 'A behavioral approach to the rational choice theory of collective action: Presidential address, American Political Science Association, 1997.' *American Political Science Review* (American Political Science Association via JSTOR)

Ostrom, Elinor (June 2010). 'Beyond markets and states: polycentric governance of complex economic systems'. *American Economic Review* (American Economic Association)

Public Accounts Committee (February 2014) Forty-Seventh Report 'Contracting out public services to the private sector'. Parliament, London

3. Everything you know about management is wrong

Simon Caulkin

Management works, sort of. It's quite good at some things, like routine production; supermarket shelves are stocked. And the trains get there, in the end. But it's hopelessly clunky at other things, like service – and crucially, unlike the physical or medical sciences, it never gets much better. there's just more of it. The charge sheet of basic management discontents is long. Gary Hamel (2016) has estimated at $3tr the dead weight of bureaucracy carried by US companies alone. Companies in the UK and US are on investment and innovation strike, preferring instead to distribute almost all their earnings to shareholders via dividends and share buybacks (Christensen, 2012; Lazonick, 2014) – which leads some economists to posit that the era of growth is over (Gordon, 2016). They are rushing to jettison their pension obligations, and now jobs are going the same way as careers before them. At the same time, big companies are, on the whole, pretty unpleasant places to work (Birkinshaw, 2012) – engagement levels are disastrously low, and most people would rather do anything other than talk to their manager. Externally, levels of trust in business and management are no higher than can be found internally. And no wonder: the crash of 2008, the latest in a line of business scandals of increasing size and frequency, was entirely management made, a chamber of horror of errors in which top bank executives got everything wrong, from risk to resource allocation, remuneration to protection of their own equity.

Things are no brighter in the public sector, unsurprisingly, because it has been forced to adopt much the same thinking as the private sector (see John Seddon on the New Public Management in this collection). Except for a few organisations, brave and obstinate enough to challenge conventional 'best practice', most public services underperform as consistently as UK industry, with results as debilitating for the public sphere as for the economy as a whole. Mass-produced, lowest-common-denominator services are reflected in civic disengagement; uncoordinated effort, perverted purpose and perpetual crisis all too often leave suppliers demoralised and those they serve locked in dependency rather than the reverse. Many public services in today's form are a disservice to civil society.

Yet despite this catalogue of underachievement the orthodoxy maintains an iron grip. Its starting assumptions allow no alternative. It's not management's fault, it's ours. We just need to try harder. Hence the almost mystical faith, despite all the evidence, in promises of 'transformation' to be achieved by this or that management fad, most recently in the shape of Big Data, analytics and massive computing power. It is as George Monbiot describes in the foreword: '...*so pervasive, so internalised have those assumptions become that we do not even recognise them for what they are.*' Management is a fact of life. In a famous passage, J.M Keynes explained it like this. '*The ideas of economists and political philosophers, both when they are right and when they are wrong, are more powerful than is commonly understood. Indeed, the world is ruled by little else. Practical men, who believe themselves to be quite exempt from any intellectual influences, are usually the slaves of some defunct economist... Soon or late, it is ideas, not vested interests, which are dangerous for good or evil.*'

An economic theory of management

Keynes might have had management in mind. The heresy is that the current management orthodoxy is not God-given nor a biological law, like Darwin's. Nor, more surprisingly, is this practical discipline a practical, empirically derived construct. As London Business School's late Sumantra Ghoshal lamented, we do not have a managerial theory of management. It is management as seen through the eyes of academic economists, some defunct, some not. The Anglo-US model, taught in business schools and propagated by consultancies all round the world, is not about 'what works'; it is about 'what works given certain fundamental assumptions'. In effect, it is a classic exercise in game theory, in which economists, in John Kay's words, have deftly substitut[ed] a problem their methods can solve for the problem we actually face.

For management to work, the following assumptions would need to be true:

- Humans are *homo economicus*, rational utility maximisers solely actuated by self-interest. (The great economist Amartya Sen exemplified *homo economicus* thus: "Can you direct me to the railway station?" asks the stranger. "Certainly," says the local, pointing in the opposite direction, towards the post office, "and would you post this letter for me on your way?" "Naturally," says the stranger, resolving to open it to see if it contains anything worth stealing.)

- The preferred medium of economic exchange is the market. The company or organisation is a poor second-best option—'a continuation of market relations, by other means,' as one writer has put it.

- The company is the property of shareholders, and its sole purpose is to maximise their returns.

The management model we know today is an elaborate deduction from these abstract general principles. Everything else follows from them. Thus the job of managers is to make money for shareholders. But managers, like everyone else being self-interested, will empire build or otherwise assert their own interests unless they are firmly aligned through incentives and sanctions behind those of shareholders. This is the so-called 'agency problem', and agency theory is at the heart of the City governance codes that have been developed over the last 25 years (Financial Reporting Council, 2016). Strikingly, governance 'best practice' – the separation of CEO and chairman roles, a strong presence of non-execs on the board, an audit committee of non-execs – puts as much or more emphasis on preventing executive misbehaviour as on promoting the success of the company as a whole.

Individual workers below top level management will have little idea about how to contribute directly to the purpose of maximising shareholder value (in any case it is a notoriously poor motivator), so they will need to be told what to do. Hierarchy is therefore management's organising principle, embodied in performance management systems devised to monitor and control individual performance at each level. Even if shareholder value did motivate, it would always be trumped by self-interest. So, reward has to be with crude carrot and stick, i.e. extrinsic rather than intrinsic to the job. Hence the ubiquity of incentives and performance-related pay – wildly elaborate at board and top management level – contingent on meeting an array of targets, whether around financial ratios, budgets, sales, service-level agreements or standards or the performance of subordinates. Internal (and external) competition decides how people at all levels get on.

Invalid prescriptions based on false assumptions.

The trouble is that all three of the founding assumptions on which the edifice of management rests are unrealistic at best; nor are they supported by evidence that they work in practice.

We can accept that self-interest is built into human nature. It is part of the mechanism of survival. But very few people are wholly self-interested (and those that are are often found in business – on which important topic more later). Otherwise there would be no Wikipedia, no open-source software (and thus no internet), no Médicins Sans Frontieres, no voluntary service, and we wouldn't tip waiters or taxi drivers whom we will never see again. Altruism also exists and is as much part of human nature as self-interest. *Homo economicus* – the individual unit of management – is a travesty of human nature.

Second, companies aren't an inferior alternative to the market. In the ecology of a dynamic, well-functioning economy, companies and markets are separate but interdependent entities, each with its own distinct role and logic.

In brief, markets dispose, companies propose. Markets are blind, impersonal and unintentional. Their domain is static efficiencies, that is, ensuring the most efficient use of existing resources by competing away temporary advantage and handing on the benefit to consumers and society. Take taxi-ride platform Uber. As the Global McKinsey Institute (2016) has pointed out, Uber destroys more value than it creates, with the difference handed on to passengers in the shape of cheaper, more convenient rides. The market favours Uber. Companies, on the other hand, are intentional organisations. Unlike markets, they can scheme and strategise. In effect, companies are a shelter from markets from which managers can plot to take one step back – forego present efficiencies – in order to make a much bigger leap forward in the future by creating altogether new resources.

That is why companies carry out R&D or allow individuals to spend part of their time on their own projects, as at Google or 3M. Companies create dynamic efficiencies through innovation, something markets can't do; markets winnow out the good from the bad and generalise the benefits. Markets and companies are different but complementary. The perennial urge to increase efficiency by making companies more market-like is thus both wrong-headed and counterproductive – it undermines the point of having the company in the first place.

Finally, shareholders do not own companies – they own shares in companies, which give them certain rights, such as electing directors, and to residual cash flows. The difference is more than semantic. Companies are independent legal entities and, as legal scholars such as Lynn Stout (2012) have demonstrated, it is to the company that directors owe their fiduciary duty, not the shareholders. The corollary of shareholder ownership, the requirement to maximise shareholder value (MSV) is equally unsustainable, either in theory or common sense. Ironically, shareholder value doesn't serve shareholders very well. In Built to Last, Jim Collins and Jerry Porras (1994) found that companies that had a purpose beyond making money for shareholders did better than shareholder-value fundamentalist peers. That finding was replicated more recently by Roger Martin (2011), then dean of Toronto's Rotman School of Management, who showed that in the era of shareholder primacy from the 1970s to the present, shareholders had done worse than in the previous 'managerialist' period when managers were supposedly feathering their own nests. This chimes with research showing that governance prescriptions, such as separating the roles of chairman and CEO or increasing the presence of non-executive directors, have little effect on company performance (even reportedly the reverse in financial institutions during the Great Crash of 2008), and – not for want of trying – no one has ever found a convincing link between superior performance and soaring CEO pay. In short, MSV doesn't work in its own terms, while its dis-benefits, many held up to unforgiving light in the Great Crash, are more manifest by the day. It would be hard to find a reputable commentator nowadays who would argue the contrary.

Doing the wrong thing righter

If all the founding assumptions of management are wrong, the questions that troubled me as I wrote weekly management columns for The Observer – Why did so much of this much-studied, apparently practical discipline appear to do the opposite of what it said on the tin? Why was it, as Peter Drucker lamented, that 'so much of management consists of making it difficult for people to work'? – were suddenly answered. Or rather, they were reversed. The issue was no longer why so much of management was wrong – it was how could anything dependent on such false premises be right?

It can't. Everything we think we know about management is wrong. Force-fitting humanity's crooked timber into the clean right angles of a mathematical abstraction is a recipe for failure. 'Bad Management Theories Are Destroying Good Management Practices', Ghoshal summed it up in the title of his posthumously published 2005 essay. Here is the reason management never progresses: it is a system, and if the system is set up to do the wrong thing, no amount of tinkering with the parts will make it work better. On the contrary, as in Russell Ackoff's much quoted diagnosis: 'Most systems pursue objectives other than those they proclaim. They try to do the wrong thing righter and this makes what they do wronger. It is much better to do the right thing wrong than the wrong thing right because when errors are corrected it makes doing the wrong things wronger, but the right things righter.'

The current version of management is a classic case of doing the wrong thing righter, acting on the parts and further destabilising the whole. This is what regulation is, as is performance management and CSR; new rules pile up and make it ever harder for people to work. Look no further for the reason for Hamel's obstinate bureaucracy and the ever-growing number of what David Graeber (2013) calls 'bullshit jobs'– meaningless compliance, assessment and checking work detested by those who do it, work that is not coincidentally concentrated in managerial, professional and clerical occupations. At the extreme, organisations subject to the demands of today's management bureaucracy can become their psychopathic opposites, the reversed-out versions of themselves: banks that make people poorer, hospitals that kill patients, public services that destroy community rather than reinforce it.

The fact that it's an interlocking system is one reason that management is so hard to change. It's impossible to do so incrementally. Unless the underlying assumptions change, nothing does. Pace Keynes, powerful vested interests and deeply internalised conventional wisdom combine to freeze things as they are.

How beliefs create their own reality

There's another powerful reason, already alluded to in passing, why unfreezing management is getting both more difficult and more urgent. This is the phenomenon of the self-fulfilling prophecy – the mechanism, unique to human affairs (and entirely untranslatable into economists' equations), by which theories or beliefs evoke behaviour that in effect makes them come true, even if they were originally false. The exemplary case is economics. for example, most people would probably agree that *homo economicus* is a reductive, one-dimensional representation of human nature. But there is plenty of evidence that the more people are exposed to the notion that it is the norm, the more they come to accept that they should believe it too. Summing it up in an academic paper, Jeff Pfeffer (2005) and others wrote: There is a growing body of evidence that self-interested behaviour is learned behaviour, and it is learned by studying business and economics. Business and economics courses, he added less academically, are a hazard to your moral health.

The implications of this are momentous. Social science theory matters more than most people suppose, perhaps even Keynes. The ability of beliefs to create their own reality means that getting management right, or at least on the right path, is not simply a practical matter of improving the social technology of common achievement. How it is 'improved' will itself be conditioned by the unspoken assumptions about corporate purpose and human motivation. For example, current discussions about automation and the future of work assume that outcomes will be determined by the interplay of an unstoppable technological imperative with the equally unstoppable economic imperative of globalisation. Entirely omitted from the calculation is any recognition that the 'gig economy' did not emerge out of the blue: it is just another manifestation, following downsizing, outsourcing and the end of career, of managers' ongoing determination to make their companies more like markets, itself (again) the product of a belief system based on assumptions about human nature and shareholder primacy. In this way, notes Pfeffer, management practices truly do become self-fulfilling, as they produce the very attitudes and behaviours that make the practices necessary and justified.

A 'good' theory of management

We badly need a new theory and model of management that is 'good' in both senses of the word. Reversing the current starting assumptions is a sensible starting point. Without being po-faced, it needs to incorporate more rounded assumptions about human nature, allowing trust and intrinsic motivation to become as self-reinforcing as greed and suspicion currently are; recognition of the need to nourish the unique properties of the company; and the obvious and observable notion that a company thrives when it simultaneously pays attention to the interests of employees, customers, suppliers and shareholders, and thereby those of the wider community too.

If it is to improve on the doubly-bad version we are saddled with at the moment, a managerial theory of management must also be good, in its other sense of empirical validation, at being able to illuminate and explain. The cheering thing is that by now we do know quite a lot about what really works – it is just that the evidence has been brushed aside or ignored by the mainstream because it refuses to fit the accepted narrative. Thus in almost every industry there is at least one 'positive deviant', a company that survives and prospers using the same resources as its conventional competitors but in very different ways. Notable examples include Apple, Toyota, Handelsbanken, W.L. Gore, Whole Foods Markets, and Berkshire Hathaway. Disparate as they are all these companies reflect more positive, less instrumental assumptions about people and business. All recognise, or intuit, that organisations are systems that can only be optimised as a whole. All know the limits of command-and-control. All use the systemic relationship between customer purpose and measures relating to that purpose to free up their front lines to innovate with method. All know that success can only be judged in the long term. Beneath the radar, there are many much smaller organisations in the public sector similarly outperforming their conventional peers, sometimes by orders of magnitude, each constituting a node of both resistance and hope for the future.

As for the responsibility for change, resistance and hope are fractal: it belongs to everyone who works in an organisation. 'Our beliefs about human nature help shape human nature itself', wrote the psychologist Robert Frank. At present, as embodied in current management models, they are in danger of turning us into travesties of human beings: stunted economic actors who are expected to leave moral, ethical and even generous impulses at the door. This is not inevitable. But it does mean that resistance and hope are all our concern. For mankind as well as management, the choice of what we believe in and stand up for at work is one of the most important we can make.

References

Birkinshaw, J. (2012) *Reinventing Management* (Revised and Updated Edition), Jossey-Bass

Christensen, C. (2012) 'A Capitalist's Dilemma, Whoever Wins on Tuesday', *New York Times*, 4/11/2012

Collins, J., Porras, J. (1994) *Built To Last: Successful Habits of Visionary Companies*, Random House

Davis, G. (2016) *The Vanishing American Corporation: Navigating the Hazards of a New Economy*, Berrett-Koehler Publishers

Ferraro, F., Pfeffer, J., Sutton, R. (2005) Economics Language and Assumptions: How Theories Can Become Self-fulfilling, *Academy of Management Review*, Vol. 30, No.1, pp.8-24.

Financial Reporting Council, 2016. The UK Corporate Governance Code, FRC

Ghoshal, S. (2005) 'Bad Management Theories Are Destroying Good Management Practices'. *Academy of Management Learning & Education*, Vol. 4, No. 1, pp.75-91.

Gordon, R. (2016) *The Rise and Fall of American Growth*, Princeton University Press

Graeber, D. (2013) 'On the Phenomenon of Bullshit Jobs', *Strike! Magazine*, [Online] http://strikemag.org/bullshit-jobs. [Accessed 3/11/2016]

Hamel, G., and Zanini, M. (2016) 'Excess Management Is Costing the U.S. $3 Trillion Per Year'. *Harvard Business Review Digital Article*, [Online] https://hbr.org/2016/09/excess-management-is-costing-the-us-3-trillion-per-year. [Accessed 3/11/2016]

Lazonick, W. (2014) 'Profits Without Prosperity'. *Harvard Business Review*, September

McKinsey Global Institute (2016) 'Independent Work: Choice, necessity and the gig economy', *MGI*, October

Martin, R. (2011) *Fixing the Game*, Harvard Business Review Press

Stout, L. (2012) *The Shareholder Value Myth: How Putting Shareholders First Harms Corporations, Investors, and the Public*, Berrett-Koehler Publisher

4. Outcome-Based Performance Management makes things worse

Toby Lowe

The orthodoxy I am challenging is the belief that measuring 'outcomes' of initiatives or interventions is an effective way to manage the performance of people and organisations who deliver social initiatives or interventions. This is known as Outcome-Based Performance Management (OBPM) and is used to evaluate a range of social and public policy activities, including education, employability programmes, health and social care, and the rehabilitation of offenders.

The orthodoxy states that those delivering such activities should be held accountable for the results of their activities – for the 'outcomes' that are produced as a consequence of the work that they do, as felt by the beneficiaries of that work and by society as a whole. This stems from a desire to ensure that social interventions improve the lives of the people they are supposed to help.

> Outcome-based government means focusing on those initiatives that genuinely change people's lives: more often than not, tackling root causes rather than simply treating symptoms. Spending is most worthwhile, for example, when it ensures addicts are freed from their addiction, no longer committing crime to fund their habit, and gainfully employed; when it ensures prisoners are rehabilitated so that they do not reoffend, but instead contribute to society; and when vulnerable families are guided and supported to ensure that children grow up stable, and able to fulfil their potential. Changing life outcomes can improve the lives of individuals and their communities, resulting in savings to taxpayers.
>
> (Centre for Social Justice, Outcomes Based-Government, 2011)

The purest form of OBPM is Payment by Results (PbR). This is a form of performance management in which those who deliver social interventions only get paid if they deliver agreed outcomes. According to the theory, PbR focusses the organisation on delivering good, effective services:

> ...it is not enough to pay someone to provide a service with the only recourse being that if they fail they will not be re-awarded the contract. In these cases, it makes sense to build in an element of payment by results to provide a constant and tough financial incentive for providers to deliver good services throughout the term of the contract. This approach will encourage providers to work more closely

with citizens and communities to build services that are both more
efficient and qualitatively different, orientated around individuals and
communities in ways that foster mutual support, respect and, where
possible, self-help.

(Cabinet Office, Open Public Services White Paper, 2011)

This orthodoxy is held by governments across the world, including
the USA, Canada, Great Britain and Australia (Halligan 2012), at both
national, regional and local levels. In the United Kingdom, at a national
level the Payment by Results approach has been used to performance-
manage employment programmes (the Work Programme), the
rehabilitation of offenders (Transforming Rehabilitation) and provides
the conceptual framework for the new wave of Social Impact Bond
programmes (Centre for Social Impact Bonds, 2015).

Support bodies for governments at all levels have produced reports that
promote the use of OBPM approaches. The World Bank has produced
a 'how-to' guide, encouraging all governments to adopt the approach
(Perrin, 2006). In the UK, the Local Government Information Unit
(LGIU) has produced a 'how to' guide for Local Government, encouraging
local authorities to adopt the approach for care for vulnerable adults
(LGIU, 2012).

The thinking behind OBPM is supported by a range of academics,
think-tanks and consultancies. Notable contributions in the area have
been made by Robert Schalock (1995) in his work on Outcomes-Based
Evaluation, Mark Friedman (2001) through his Outcomes-Based
Accountability™ programme (also known as Results-Based Accountability
in other countries) and through think-tanks in UK such as the Centre for
Social Justice (2011).

Heresy

My heresy is simple: OBPM makes social interventions worse, not better.
Measuring 'outcomes' cannot be used to performance manage the delivery
of social interventions without distorting and corrupting the practices it
intends to manage. This is the paradox of outcomes (Lowe, 2013). If you
try to use 'outcomes' as a mechanism for performance management for
social interventions, it creates worse outcomes, particularly for those with
the most complex needs. This is particularly true of its most pernicious
form, Payment by Results.

OBPM seeks to create accountability for delivering good results. In
reality, it does the opposite. It corrupts the purpose of those who deliver
social interventions, turning them from people whose job it is to help
others, into people whose job it is to produce good-looking data showing
positive results. It turns the practice of delivering social interventions into

a game: a game that is won by those who are good at producing data, not by those who are good at helping others to achieve their goals.

My heresy is an elaboration of Cambell's Law. Donald Campbell (1976) in his essay 'Assessing the impact of planned social change' wrote

> The more any quantitative social indicator is used for social decision-making, the more subject it will be to corruption pressures and the more apt it will be to distort and corrupt the social processes it is intended to monitor.

It is extremely frustrating that this needs repeating in 2015. We have known since 1976 that OBPM makes things worse and not better. We have spent nearly 40 years unnecessarily pursuing a management philosophy which harms those who need help most by corrupting the practice of those whose job it is to help them.

The orthodoxy is wrong because the evidence about what happens when people implement OBPM approaches clearly indicates a corruption of practice – the creation of a game whose rules favour a form of gamesmanship that makes people produce data rather than help those in need. Whenever an in-depth study is undertaken which examines the impact on practice of OBPM approaches, it produces similar results. These results are summed up by Erica Wimbush (2011):

> The overall conclusion from international experience of implementing an outcomes approach is that the journey is long and the results are disappointing.

'Disappointing' is far too mild a word to use. The evidence from research interviews with managers and practitioners who operate under OBPM regimes is profoundly shocking. A recent example of such research is Soss, Fording & Schram (2011). They conducted a detailed study of the behaviour and perspectives of officials, managers and staff delivering the Temporary Assistance for Needy Families (TANF) programme in the United States. This programme is commissioned and performance-managed using a PbR framework which disciplines all those involved with the programme, both staff and those in receipt of support.

They found that the OBPM regime focuses staff time on the production of data, rather than supporting clients (Soss, Fording & Schram 2011: 221):

> **Regional Official A**: You don't hire a "people person" anymore for a career manager position. You hire a clerical computer person. You can teach them the social work stuff easily. The job's all about time, accuracy, and files now. There's a person [client] down there somewhere. But the technical stuff is what matters.

> **State Official**: What you're telling me is the [information] systems are driving the [case management] process.

Several Regional Officials: *Oh yes. Oh yes!*

Regional Official B: *You don't get any credit [in the performance measures] for hand-holding. You don't get any credit for mentoring. [...]*

Regional Official C: *If you talk to any case manager here, they will tell you they're not a case manager; they're a technician. They spend about 10 percent of their time on their clients. Their time is about being a technician, and that's the way the program is written. They're doing what they have to do under this system.*

A similar picture was found in a study of the implementation of Results Based Accountability™ in Australia (Keevers *et al.* 2012). This study is significant because it is one of the few which has undertaken an in-depth 'before and after' look at how the introduction of Results Based Accountability affects the practices of frontline staff within social support organisations. It found that staff spend time collecting and analysing data about young people rather than spending time developing and maintaining the quality of relationships which are the cornerstone of their work with young people.

The negative effects of the OBPM regime can clearly be seen from the way in which the workers describe its impact on their practice:

> *It's constantly looking at numbers. Yeah, and the quality and depth of the client contact has really declined in the last couple of months because of the pressure of the new data and monitoring requirements. We don't get the funding unless we meet the targets. It's really changed the way we work. ... If a young person was having problems with transport or anything like that we would go and meet the client. We would either go to where they were staying and do the assessment there, or we'd take them somewhere where they felt more comfortable, so we might meet them at McDonalds or something like that. Now we can't – we can't do any of that because we have to enter information onto the computer as soon as they come in. And they [funding body] have either booked us an appointment right after or there is not enough space between times to drop them off and pick them up. (reflective discussion).* (Keevers at al 2012:114)

Such accounts of the way in which OBPM regimes serve to shape the thinking of those who work under them add depth and detail to other research with staff at all levels who have been involved with OBPM mechanisms. Together, this research suggests that in order to produce the required data, people 'game the system' in various ways: creaming & parking, teaching to the test, reclassifying, and falsification of data. These studies find this same 'gaming' activity in a huge variety of policy settings, across a range of different places (Bevan & Hood 2006b – UK, Health Service; Perrin 1998 – USA and Canada, employment programmes; van Theeil & Leuww 2002 – Europe & USA, public services; Rothstein 2008 – USA, education; Newton 2012: UK, employment programmes).

The effects are summarised by Burt Perrin (1998), who says that targets frequently distort the direction of programs, diverting attention away from, rather than towards, what the program should be doing.

The conclusion that we are able to draw from this range of research is that, when interviewed, managers and staff from a range of policy contexts across the world tell remarkably similar stories about the way in which OBPM impacts on their practice and shapes their thinking. This impact is to the detriment of the quality and effectiveness of the services that they are delivering. And each time this occurs, it is the clients, those people most in need of support, who suffer.

What has to change,?

We have seen what the impacts of OBPM are. Most of the evidence of problems highlighted in the previous section is not new. So, given that these problems are known, what has the response been?

Unfortunately, the response has been to view the issues as technical problems about measurement and suggestions for improvement have been to change the measures, or the way in which measurement is done (see for example: Perrin 1998, Mayne 2007 or Rothstein 2008). But the problems are not technical problems about measurement – they cannot be solved by new measures, or new ways of measurement. These problems are the result of flawed theory – they are intrinsic to the nature of OBPM, as we shall now explore.

Flawed theory

OBPM corrupts practice for two reasons, both of which are related to the requirement to simplify the complex nature of reality:

1. It pretends it is measuring outcomes in people's lives, but it doesn't, because it is far too expensive and resource intensive to do so

2. It pretends that outcomes are caused by particular interventions, when in reality outcomes are the result of the workings of complex systems.

We will look at each of these in turn.

The Measurement Problem

One clear and compelling answer to the question of "Why measure outcomes?" is: "To see if programs really make a difference in the lives of people." (United Way of America, 1996)

Unfortunately, it turns out that it is far too difficult to measure the difference a social intervention makes in someone's life. According to Schalock, the father of outcome evaluation, you have to have a very exacting research methodology which involves control groups, qualitative and quantitative methods, participant involvement in research design and a minimum post-programme follow-up study of at least 22 months (Schalock 2001). This is extremely resource intensive. When Campbell (1976) studied the impact of the introduction of a minimum-income guarantee to 300 households in the USA, the intervention itself cost $3 million to deliver. The accompanying outcome-research cost $5 million.

Consequently, in practice, no-one does genuine outcome-evaluation for the purpose of performance management – you cannot manage programmes in real time based on information that you have to wait a minimum of 22 months to collect, and that might cost almost twice to collect as much as the programme itself does to deliver. Therefore, OBPM uses proxy measures. This is what Mark Friedman (2001) observes:

> If we had a thousand measures, we could still not fully capture the health and readiness of young children. We use data to approximate these conditions and to stand as proxies for them.

Similarly, Russell Webster (2014) a writer and thinker on Payment by Results, suggests the following commandments when developing metrics for Payment by Results programmes:

> Commandment 2: Thy outcomes shall be few.
> Commandment 3: Thy metrics shall be simple.

The problem for OBPM is that reality is complex and messy – and therefore difficult and expensive to measure. OBPM requires simple metrics by which to make judgements about whether a social intervention has created the desired impact in people's lives. It takes the complexity of reality, and abstracts away the complexity until it is left with something which is easy and cheap to measure. Unfortunately, this means it is no longer measuring the reality of outcomes, it is measuring what is measurable, and calling that an outcome.

A classic example of this in practice is the use of Body Mass Index (BMI) as a proxy measure for obesity. The National Obesity Observatory (2009) states: true measures of body fat are impractical or expensive to use, and therefore BMI is an attractive measure because it is an easy, cheap and non-invasive means of assessing excess body fat.

Unfortunately, because BMI's use as a performance measure is problematic:

> BMI is only a proxy indicator of body fatness; factors such as fitness (muscle mass), ethnic origin and puberty can alter the relationship between BMI and body fatness. Therefore, BMI may not be an accurate tool for assessing weight status at an individual level, and other ways of measuring body composition may be more useful and accurate.   (National Obesity Observatory, 2009, p. 3)

But because it is easy to measure, it is used as a performance management metric.

Rochdale's public health strategy is just one of many Local Authorities in the UK to use BMI as a performance management metric. Between 2010 and 2015, it set a target of reducing the percentage of the population in the 'overweight' category of BMI (BMI scores of 26-30) from 56.5% to 45%, and the 'obese' (BMI scores of more than 30) from 20.8% of the population to 16%.

What happens, then, when these proxy measures are used for performance management? The answer is that they corrupt the practice of those who deliver interventions designed to address the issue of obesity.

The story of Anita Albrecht is instructive at this point (Metro, 2014). She was a personal trainer and bodybuilder who, in 2014, went for a routine appointment with a nurse. The nurse measured her BMI, and found that it was 29 – in the overweight category, and only one point short of obesity. The nurse told Anita that she should go on a calorie-controlled diet, and that she should take more exercise! A nurse told a personal trainer to take more exercise, on the basis of her BMI score! Because she was looking only at a proxy measure – at a simplified, abstracted version of Anita – the kind of image you see on obesity charts – and treated Anita accordingly.

When human beings, with complex lives, are treated as pieces of proxy data by OBPM, it simplifies the reality of the complex outcomes they seek, and turns them into pale abstractions of themselves. This is true for all outcome proxy measures: an employment programme that only measures whether someone is in work or not fails to understand the complexity of a real job in their life. For an unemployed person, is having a job automatically better than not having one? What if they suffer from fragile mental health, and the stress of a bad job gives them a relapse? What if they are caring for a dependent relative with the time that they would otherwise spend working? What if they are volunteering in their community with that time? If, as OBPM states, it genuinely wants to see if programs make a difference, it would explore all of these issues. A simple proxy measure cannot.

The Attribution Problem

The second simplification problem faced by OBPM is that it seeks to attribute effects (outcomes) to causes (interventions) in a linear fashion – if we do X to group Y, then we will get outcome Z. We can see this thinking in the 'program logic models' which are the recommended way of thinking about how outcomes are created. This version is from Schalock and Bonham (2003):

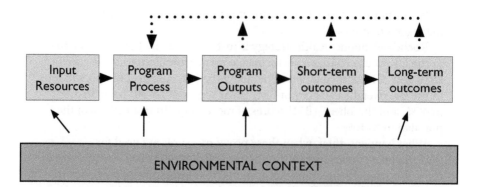

This linear thinking is intrinsic to OBPM because it seeks to identify accountability for delivering outcomes. It rewards or punishes organisations (or programmes, teams or people) based on measured outcomes. And, in the case of Payment by Results, it pays organisations based on the whether the data says these outcomes have been achieved.

And so, in order, to know who to pay, and how much to pay them, the measured outcomes must relate to particular interventions (the inputs and process in the above diagram).For OBPM to function, outcomes must be the product of identifiable interventions – otherwise there is no accountability, and no-one to pay!

But outcomes are not created in this linear way. Outcomes are created by an enormous range of factors. These factors are part of complex systems – meaning that they interact with each other, and with the system as a whole, in ways which cannot be predicted from the starting conditions of that system.

We can illustrate this idea using the systems map of obesity. This was produced by Vandenbroeck for the Government Office for Science in 2007 and is shown on the next page. It maps all the factors which lead to obesity:

As we can see, there are hundreds of factors identified on the map. Some of these factors are under the control of the delivery organisation, some of which they can influence, many of which they can't control or influence.

Furthermore, because of the complex ways in which these factors interact with each other, and with the system as a whole, the results of this system – the outcomes – cannot be predicted from the starting conditions. Such systems are described as non-linear, meaning *a system whose output is not proportional to its input… Here we can have changes in effects which are disproportionate to changes in the causal elements(s). Such systems exhibit general deterministic chaos where very small variations in the input parameters can generate very different output values in a system of equations* (Byrne & Callaghan, 2014).

Foresight
Obesity System Map

This means that outcomes are emergent properties of complex systems. They are not under the control of organisations which deliver social interventions. Consequently, OBPM is seeking to hold people and organisations accountable for things that they cannot control.

What this means is that if you are working in one area of the system – say you are working with people to address their activity levels and food consumption – the outcomes for the people with whom you work (whether they are obese or not) are determined by an enormous range of things that are beyond your control. You may deliver a fantastic programme that works to address the key aspects of an individual's attitude to exercise and eating, but the person has to take on an extra job in order to make ends meet, meaning they don't have time to cook properly. Or their relationship ends, and they began to comfort eat. Or bodybuilding is their hobby, meaning their BMI is high no matter how they eat or exercise.

Similarly, if your organisation delivers a brilliant employability programme with an incredible track record of helping people find employment, and then the economy crashes, the number of people who find work will drastically reduce. If your organisation is being paid on the basis of these results, this creates enormous problems.

The root of these problems is, once more, OBPM's desire to simplify. In order to hold people and organisations accountable for producing desired results, it must pretend that the world is more simple than it is. It must pretend that particular social interventions produce particular outcomes, instead of acknowledging that outcomes are actually emergent properties of complex systems.

Unpicking the theoretical assumptions which underpin OBPM enables us to identify that OBPM faces two key problems (1) most outcomes cannot be authentically measured without incurring prohibitive costs and (2) outcomes are not created by, nor attributable to, particular interventions. At the root of both of these problems is a failure to accept the complexity of life as it is lived by real people

The process of simplification and abstraction turns the complex reality of life into a simple game (analogous to the way in which a game such as Monopoly is a simple abstraction from real-life capitalism). In order to succeed at the OBPM game people are required to produce the appropriate performance data. Those who produce the appropriate data are rewarded, those who fail to do so are punished.

The desired purpose behind OBPM is to encourage those who deliver under such regimes to produce appropriate performance data by providing effective services to those they support. However, the way in which the rules of OBPM game are constructed does not favour this way of playing. Instead, the rules favour a different set of tactics.

The process of simplification pretends that what is measured is an 'outcome', and that such 'outcomes' are under the control of those who are being held accountable for delivering them. However, those playing the game at the frontline necessarily engage with reality. They know that the genuine impact of the programme is not being captured by proxy measures, and that outcomes are emergent properties of complex systems. Those confronted with the disconnect between OBPM's simplified rules and the complex reality of life must find tactics to reconcile the two. Sometimes they struggle with this:

> *They say that we're not, how would you say it . . . a social service agency in a sense, like we're a business . . . But at the same time . . . you're working with people who have needs, who have barriers, and bringing the two together is very difficult. [. . .] There's a number game that we have to play. And when you bring that into it, it's hard for me to sit with an individual there; they're telling me that they have all these barriers. For example, they're coming in and they're telling me that they've been evicted from their apartment, they don't have any place to live, they don't have any food, they don't have any clothes. And then here I am as a case manager you have to participate at 40 hours a week. You know, it's just kind of, it's crazy!'*
> (Soss, Fording and Schram, 2011: 220)

While RBA planning tools offer simplification and standardization for some stakeholders, such tools can create confusion and dilemmas for others (Bowker & Star, 1999, p. 293). Practitioners from community organizations struggled to work out how to account for the importance of relationships within RBA planning practices (Keevers *et al* 2012: 109).

As a consequence of being held accountable for outcomes which are beyond their control, staff who are involved with the development and delivery of social interventions learn to manage what they can control, which is the production of data. We can see this exemplified in the evidence gathered:

> *Finally, when local actors respond to performance pressures, they also confront 'easy versus hard' paths when deciding whether to focus on improving serve to the existing client pool or, alternatively, selecting a client pool that will make it easier to meet performance goals. Evidence from all regions in this study suggests that the latter path is usually seen as easier. Accordingly, creative efforts to innovate are often directed toward reshaping the clientele rather than serving them more effectively.*
>
> *In the WT program, serious reforms designed to deal with problems of poverty and work are (not surprisingly) often viewed as difficult to achieve, and their performance effects are usually seen as distant and*

uncertain. It is far easier to change how one classifies existing activities and count measured behaviours. As a result, as one local official told us forthrightly, "people game the numbers all the time." In describing efforts to meet the required participation rate, another regional official explained: "You have to do all sorts of things to fill the participation hours. We've got a client who we found out was taking her pastor to church on Sunday. We went out and asked her pastor to sign on saying this was community service. The trick is to find out what people are already doing and find a way to count it as work or community service. This is how you have to do it."(p.209/10)

We can model this behaviour to examine the drivers behind the development of this particular set of tactics for playing the OBPM game. This model begins to explore the rational drivers underpinning the development of tactics needed to play the OBPM game well. The diagram below (Lowe and Wilson 2015) examines the choices faced by staff by placing them along two axes. Along the horizontal axis staff can judge the probability of whether their choices will create an improvement in the results data. The vertical axis concerns the cost of adjustments that they can make. Some changes that they make will be expensive to implement. Others will be cheaper .

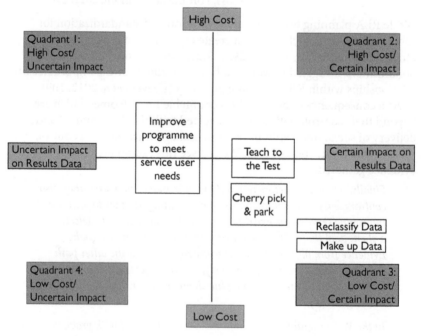

The quadrant that staff will rationally seek to occupy will be the quadrant in which the changes they make will have the greatest likelihood of producing the required data, and those which will be cheapest to implement. Hence, Quadrant 3: Low Cost/Certain Impact is the most desirable. These are the choices that will result in the organisation achieving the best financial return and which will keep the overall cost of programme competitive against other organisations that will be tendering for this work.

We can see that all the choices that exist in the 'best' quadrant (3) are those that involve 'gaming' the system. The drivers for making these choices are felt keenly by staff:

> The stress felt by case managers can be traced partly to their belief
> that performance numbers matter for job security and trajectory. WT
> case managers make modest wages in a job with few guarantees, and
> a non-trivial number have previously received welfare themselves.
> They often struggle to make ends meet and, as a result, tend to
> view performance through the prism of their own anxieties as
> breadwinners. Few expect to be "fired" if their numbers drop. But
> in a system of for-profit contracting, most are keenly aware that
> performance numbers drive profits, and declining profits could
> lead their current employer to downsize the staff or even to sell the
> operation to another company whose retention of old employees is
> uncertain. At a less absolute level, most expect that if they produce
> weak numbers, they will be subjected to greater supervision in a way
> that will make their work more stressful and harder to do.
> (Soss, Fording and Schram, 2011: 221)

This is the nature of playing the OBPM game. The rules of the game create a rationality which favours a set of tactics that have previously been called 'gaming'. However, all those involved in the system are playing a game. The issue is not about game-playing but about the tactics different players use. A better term for such tactics would seem to be 'gamesmanship' – "the use of dubious (although not technically illegal) methods to win or gain a serious advantage in a game" (Wikipedia).

Each person within the game has to find a way to play it that responds to the underlying rationality of the rules, but which also responds to the complexity of the real world they encounter. The game therefore exists in two separate dimensions: the dimension of simplified rules, and the complex reality of life. (Imagine trying to conduct business affairs using the rules of Monopoly.) This means that the game does not 'make sense' but still staff must learn to play it well:

> "The way we're able to [stay in business and] help people is by making
> our measurements on our red and green reports and getting paid,

so that we can therefore in return help with childcare and support services [. . .] So the more we make those measurements and those goals, the more we can help candidates. But the more we focus on those [performance goals],the less we're focusing on the candidates. So, it's a catch-22." (p.211)

It is important to note that 'playing the game well' may well involve aspects of delivering the service well. It is not impossible to improve performance data by actually improving the service that is offered to clients. It is perfectly possible that this occurs, and indeed is likely to be the case in some instances, as the motivations of many of those who do this work are to help those in need:

...case managers are rarely single-minded performance maximizers. More typically, they are ambivalent actors caught in the cross-pressures of competing values, identities, and organizational forces (see also, Watkins-Hayes 2009, 2011). Despite the rhetoric of the "business model," most express a strong commitment to social service ideals and value their identities as providers who are responsive to clients' needs. As a result, they express deep reservations about making case decisions based on performance goals. (p.219)

Therefore the rational driver to develop tactics which maximise the production of good-looking data is tempered by people's values – their desire to do a good job. However, our model shows that such behaviour – actually delivering the service well – is likely to be expensive, time consuming and have an uncertain impact on the data. This is a risky tactic because others will be able to construct better-looking data, whilst expending fewer resources.

So, in order to change the tactics that people use, we must change the rules of the performance management game. We must develop a new conceptual framework for performance management which accepts the complex reality of social interventions, and which builds its conceptual framework from there.

Dr. Toby Lowe , Senior Research Associate, Business School, Newcastle University

References

Bellavita, C. (2006) *Homeland Security Affairs*, Vol. II, No.3

Byrne, D. and Callaghan, G. (2014) *Complexity Theory and the Social Sciences: the state of the art.* Routledge

Campbell, D. (1976). Assessing the Impact of Planned Social Change [pdf]. Available at <https://www.globalhivmeinfo.org/CapacityBuilding/Occasional%20Papers/08%20Assessing%20the%20Impact%20of%20Planned%20Social%20Change.pdf> Accessed 15th February 2013.

Centre for Social Impact Bonds (2015) 'Social impact bonds (SIBs): a Payment by Results model', Cabinet Office, [Online] https://data.gov.uk/sib_knowledge_box/social-impact-bonds-sibs-payment-results-model accessed 29th October 2015.

Centre for Social Justice (2011), 'Outcomes Based-Government'

Cabinet Office, Open Public Services White Paper, 2011

Friedman, M. (2001) 'Results Based Accountability Implementation Guide' [pdf]. Available at <http://www.raguide.org/>. [Accessed 28th May 2013]

Gigerenzer, G. (2014) *Risk Savvy*. Allen Lane

Halligan, J *et al* (2012),"On the road to performance governance in the public domain?", *International Journal of Productivity and Performance Management*, Vol. 61, Iss 3, pp.224-234

Keevers, L., *et al* (2012) 'Made to measure: taming practices with Results-Based Accountability.' *Organization Studies* 33,1: 97-120

Local Government Information Unit (2012), 'Outcomes Matter: Effective Commissioning in Domiciliary Care'

Lowe, T. (2013) 'The paradox of outcomes: the more we measure the less we understand', *Public Money and Management*, 33: 3, 213-216

Lowe, T. and Wilson, R. (2015) Playing the Game of Outcomes-based Performance Management. Is Gamesmanship Inevitable? Evidence from Theory and Practice, Social Policy and Administration, (epub ahead of print)

Mayne, J. (2007) 'Challenges and lessons in implementing Results-Based Management'. *Evaluation*, Vol 13, 1: 87–109.

Metro (2014) 'A picture of obesity: NHS tells bodybuilder she must lose weight and exercise more...'. http://metro.co.uk/2014/03/26/a-picture-of-obesity-nhs-tells-bodybuilder-she-must-lose-weight-and-exercise-more-4679903/

National Obesity Observatory & NHS (2009) Body Mass Index as a Measure of Obesity [pdf]. Available at http://www.noo.org.uk/uploads/doc789_40_noo_BMI.pdf. Accessed on 12th November 2013

Perrin, B. (1998) 'Effective use and misuse of Performance Measurement'. *American Journal of Evaluation*, Vol. 19, 3: 367-379

Perrin, B. (2006) *Moving from Outputs to Outcomes: Practical Advice from Governments Around the World*, World Bank and IBM Center for The Business of Government

Schalock, R. (1995 1st edition and 2001 2nd edition) *Outcomes-Based Evaluation*, Plenum

Schalock, R. & Bonham, G (2003), "Measuring outcomes and managing for results", *Evaluation and Program Planning*, 26, 4: 229-235.

Rothstein, R. (2008). Holding accountability to account: how scholarship and experience in other fields inform exploration of performance incentives in education, National Center on Performance Incentives [pdf]. Available at https://my.vanderbilt.edu/performanceincentives/files/2012/10/200804_Rothstein_HoldingAccount.pdf. Accessed on 4th February 2013.

Soss, J; Fording R; Schram, S F. (2011) 'The Organization of Discipline: From Performance Management to Perversity and Punishment', *Journal of Public Administration Research and Theory*, Vol. 21: 203-232

Thiel, S van. and Leeuw, F. L. (2002) 'The performance paradox in the public sector', *Public Performance and Management Review*, Vol 25, 3: 267-281

Vandenbroeck, P, Goossens, J. Clemens, M. (2007), Foresight Tackling Obesities: Future Choices – Building the Obesity System Map. Government Office for Science.

Webster, R. (2014) The 10 Commandments of Payment by Results: [Online] www.russellwebster.com/the-ten-commandments-of-payment-by-results/ Accessed 29th October 2015

Wimbush, E., 2011. Implementing an outcomes approach to public management and accountability in the UK—are we learning the lessons? *Public Money & Management*, Vol. 31 (3), pp.211-218

5. Government Cannot Innovate

Simon Duffy

As citizens, we get used to feeling disappointed with our government. We can also be frustrated by what we take to be its incompetence or its malign intentions. Our disappointment is shared both by those on the left, who suspect that government is the creature of capitalism, and those on the right, who prefer to put their trust in the market. It is not surprising, then, that fewer and fewer people vote, and that those who do increasingly avoid the main political parties.

The slow decline of the two party system

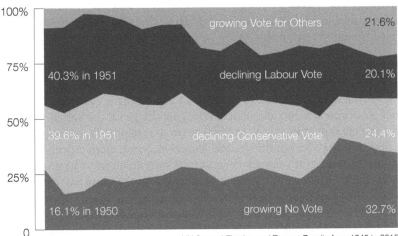

UK General Election and Turnout Results from 1945 to 2015

Of course, disappointment is what we feel when our hopes are not realised. We expect government to improve things; we hope that it will solve social problems and build a better future for its citizens. These hopes arise quite naturally, and we have entrusted government with great power and significant authority, even moral authority, to carry out this work on our behalf.

Government is run by largely intelligent and well-intentioned people; corruption is real, but not widespread, yet improvement seems very slow and things often seem to get worse. I am not suggesting that government is incompetent at administering existing systems or at maintaining law and order. These are central functions of government and are well within its powers. Our disappointment is rooted, rather, in an awareness that government is very bad at solving problems – in other words, government seems incapable of positive social innovation. As I will go on to explain, the distinction between administration and innovation is critical for understanding the limits of government's competence.

Our sense of disappointment is most likely fuelled by an orthodox belief that remains largely unchallenged; that it is the role of Government to bring about social change, to set direction and to innovate. Moreover, this belief also implies that the rest of us, the governed, are left with only the task of implementing these new policies and innovations.

Government certainly behaves as if it is responsible for innovation, although it may delegate certain tasks of creativity to think tanks, innovation units or special government departments. Local government shares the same belief, although it sees itself as a junior partner to central government. In civil society, there are organisations that try to influence or challenge policy, but only government can set policy. The media, although frequently critical of government, likewise locates the responsibility for solving problems with government. In fact, we all seem to prefer to see government as responsible, while we are mere bystanders.

Heresy

My own heresy, put crudely, is that government cannot innovate. Government is competent to govern and to administer existing systems, but government is incompetent at changing things for the better; it is incompetent at innovation. As I will go on to explain, government is crippled by its own administrative competence and, more especially, by its need to constantly appear competent. Government can't be good at everything; it is generally good at keeping things the same, but generally very bad at making things better.

Alternatively, my heresy might be stated more positively as follows. Genuine and valuable social innovations involve real and complex changes in behaviour and organizational structures. They require changes in human understanding and attitude and not just formal rule changes. Most changes cannot simply be imposed by Government; instead they must be thoughtfully developed, over time, through a process of personal, peer and social exchange. Innovation is a human and creative process and it is a process in which we can all play a valuable role.

Government's role is to create the basic framework for society – law, structure, governance and appropriate forms of redistribution of the necessary resources. However, when Government tries to push innovations itself it can damage the very thing it wants to promote. I believe it is primarily the role of citizens, not government, to innovate.

Personal budgets

To make my argument I will use one case study – the implementation of what are now called 'personal budgets'. Certainly my heresy cannot be validated by this one example but I hope that it will illuminate the factors that undermine government-driven innovations. At the very least, I hope this example will be of interest for its own sake.

Personal budgets are a new way of organising public services. Instead of citizens being offered a specific service, for example a place at a day centre, people are given a budget which they can manage and use flexibly. Management and use are not the same thing. A personal budget can be managed by the person, their representative, an intermediary or by an agent of government. Not everybody will want to take on the work of managing a personal budget: some people will need others to manage their budgets.

The purpose of a personal budget is to help someone to meet their needs in the most effective way possible; but, as individuals are all very different, personal budgets must be very flexible. Ideally it can be spent on anything that is legal, and is not limited to a narrow menu of services. Personal budgets might usefully be contrasted to vouchers. A voucher gives a person control of who will provide a specific kind of service, but the service itself is fixed. A personal budget is much more radical; it allows individuals to become innovators in their own lives and to develop the right solution for themselves. (O'Brien & Mount, 2015)

For instance, some people have used personal budgets to replace a 'meals on wheels' service. Instead of a meal being driven to their house, the citizen can ask a local pub to cook them a regular meal. This has many advantages; in particular, it strengthens personal networks, keeps money in the local economy and combines sociability with freshly cooked food.

No advocate of personal budgets claims that personal budgets can replace all public services. Many public services, for example emergency services, are best planned and managed on behalf of the whole community. Other public services, for example heart surgery, rely on expert assessments of need and an expertly controlled procedure. There is no value in converting such services into a budget for the person to manage.

A social innovation, like personal budgets, becomes useful when the person is the best agent for meeting their own needs or where the best solution for the needs can only be determined in the light of the full facts about the person's whole life and intentions. So, for example, day centres are very crude ways of helping disabled or older people to live good and meaningful lives. By their very nature they concentrate power in the institution of the centre itself, and they make it harder for people to build on their own assets or to connect to the wider community. When people have had the chance to replace a day centre with a personal budget they appear to be able to meet their needs in a more satisfactory way, by using the funding flexibly to enhance their lives. (Pitts, Soave & Waters, 2009; Hay & Waters, 2009)

Moreover, personal budgets do not need to replace those public services which people find valuable; people can choose to spend some or all of their budget on existing public services. Personal budgets are not a tool for privatising services, they are a method for strengthening people's citizenship, agency and community participation.

The emergence of personal budgets

The power of government is such that most people only get to hear about an innovation like personal budgets when the idea has already become government policy. This creates the illusion that government came up with the idea. But personal budgets were not thought out by government, rather they emerged from the long-term efforts of disabled people asserting their rights as citizens.

I developed the specific concept of personal budgets as part of my work to try and help people with learning disabilities escape institutional services, to design personalised support and to live fulfilling lives in the community (Fitzpatrick, 2010). Over time I discovered that not only was it useful to individualise funding, and shift control to people or their families, but that it was also very useful to clarify any available budget upfront. This seemed to help people plan more creatively and with a greater sense of security.

Initially I piloted these ideas at Inclusion Glasgow and then in two Scottish local authorities. In 2003, I led a project called In Control where we began piloting the system. We called it self-directed support and personal budgets were one of the key elements of this new system for social care. The approach was full of promise. People and families were more satisfied, people's active citizenship improved, and there were obvious efficiencies. As people took control of resources they made better use of them – they were more responsible and far more creative. (Glasby & Littlechild, 2009)

It was, perhaps, no surprise that this idea caught the attention of politicians and policy-makers. By 2005, 'individual budgets' had appeared in three government policies and in the 2005 Labour Party manifesto. 'Individual budgets' were later renamed, 'personal budgets' and became central to the reform of adult social care. The idea has now been extended to the NHS and to children's services. However, the reality of this policy development was far more complex.

This is not surprising. Every innovation is a disruption to an existing system so it is normal, even right, that it faces resistance. Change is not always good and government systems will certainly be defended against change. Just as there is a pattern to the evolution of innovations, so there is an evolving strategy of resistance. As innovations develop, new strategies are required to advance and develop the innovation. As innovations grow and threaten the existing system new strategies emerge in order resist or constrain the impact of the innovation. There are four stages to the development of an innovation, and likewise there are four different strategies for resistance:

1. Stage One – The primary challenge for an innovator is to realise their idea – to bring it to life.
Resistance: At this early stage the most effective strategy of resistance is to ignore the innovation, and exclude any maverick-innovator from any sphere of influence.

2. Stage Two – If an innovation is working and bringing about benefits it is possible for the innovator to make the innovation attractive, to inspire support and collaboration with others.
Resistance: The best way to resist such early support is to create a powerful negative story about the innovation, ideally using research to show that the innovation is invalid.

3. Stage Three – If an innovation continues to win support then the next stage is to make the innovation easy to use. Early forms of innovation are almost always unduly complex or burdensome (expect for those who have a very high threshold for complexity). Innovations that become successful are easy to use and feel inexpensive.
Resistance: To resist an innovation at this stage it is possible to accept the innovation as an additional option, if perhaps an unattractive one; in this way most of the system can carry on operating as before, while the innovation becomes a special option only used by a minority.

4. Stage Four – The final stage of development is for the innovation to be fully integrated into the current system.
Resistance: At this stage resistance to the innovation is best achieved by confusion and complexity, making it harder for the innovation to take hold. Strategies include renaming old processes, as if they have been newly designed to adapt to the innovations but allowing them to continue to run unchanged.

It is important to stress that this pattern of innovation and resistance involves no judgement. Although innovation might seem to be a 'good thing' it is quite possible to develop negative innovations, changes that are silly, wasteful or even wicked. Resistance is not only innate to a system, it has a positive social function. However, as we shall see, if such resistance is too powerful it can drain a positive innovation of its value.

1. Initial resistance to personal budgets

What accelerated the initial acceptance of In Control's model of personal budgets was probably a mixture of intentional strategy and dumb luck. One of the key factors was that the model was both empowering and universal and did not directly threaten public services. Everyone receiving social care could have a personal budget, but they did not have to choose any particular model of service. This made it a model that was very attractive to 'reformist' leaders within the Labour Party who were seeking something innovative, but something that would not be too threatening to allies in the trade union movement.

However, while politicians liked the idea, it soon became very clear that the role of the civil servant was to limit its impact. In fact, in the first two years of the In Control project, no civil servant ever attended one of our steering groups (although these were held inside the Department of Health). After the 2005 General Election, when Labour had included the idea in their manifesto, I was invited to explain the idea to a room full of senior civil servants whose job it was to implement and test the idea. However, I was told that I had only 10 minutes to explain something that I had spent over 10 years developing. I was also told that I must not speak during the rest of the meeting because I was not a civil servant. (I failed this second test as I could not stop myself complaining at their crazily complex plan for testing the concept.)

Finally, and most strikingly, some months after the launch of the government's own Individual Budget Pilot Programme, I was told that In Control could no longer use the term 'Individual Budget' because this was now a 'Government term'. After this, In Control changed all references in its paperwork from 'individual budget' to 'personal budget'.

It was clear of course that the civil servants did not want a maverick, with a vested interest in the innovation, having any undue influence over its implementation. However, the crazy consequence of this strategic resistance was that its own implementation plan was incoherent and incompetent.

2. Researching personal budgets

I am told that the Government's research into this innovation cost about £10 million. However, it was doomed from the very start, if not to failure, then to mediocrity. One of the most peculiar features of the project was the decision to select 13 pilot sites, and then to allow each pilot site to develop its own version of 'individual budgets', and then to pool all the data from the pilot sites so you could not see which results correlated with which model. This is not an acceptable research methodology and it is hard to resist the conclusion that it was intentionally designed to fail, or at least to give the civil servants the maximum degree of interpretational latitude at the end of the process.

However, In Control continued and began its own independent research process, working with a growing membership of over 100 local authorities. In the end, it was our development and testing of personal budgets, and our distance from the stuttering 'individual budgets' programme that actually helped Ivan Lewis, Minister for Care Services (2006-2008), to commit Government to back personal budgets.

3. Implementing personal budgets

At the end of 2007, the government published Putting People First, which declared that:

> Personal budgets [are] for everyone eligible for publicly funded adult social care support other than in circumstances where people require emergency access to provision. [HM Government, 2007]

In addition, the government committed to spend £0.5 billion over three years to implement this change. This was certainly a major shift in government policy. However, the consequences of the policy were much more ambiguous than this clear statement and the enormous financial commitment might suggest. In fact, I would suggest that nearly every penny of this money was utterly wasted.

Personal budgets were implemented because (a) people made better decisions about how to improve their lives (b) they spent money more efficiently and wisely and (c) the new system could be implemented without any additional costs. To develop the idea further required further innovation and simplification; This was not a challenge that required any additional resources. However, the impact of spending all this extra money was to attract consultancy companies to create new management roles and to fuel vanity projects. Often the original pioneers of personal budgets within local government were also ignored or replaced. The overall impact of this over-enthusiastic spending was to undermine the development of the innovation itself.

4. The end of personal budgets

Today 64% of people getting adult social care use a personal budget. However, it not clear at all that this fact reflects a substantive change in philosophy or practice (Health and Social Care Information Centre, 2015). On balance the shift to a more individualised form of funding is probably the most important long-term impact of personal budgets. In addition, 28% of people use direct payments, which means that they control their funding directly.

Many of the benefits of personal budgets have, however, been eroded. Severe cuts in funding for social care have led to local authorities reducing the flexibility of personal budgets in the name of 'cost control'. The administrative burdens of direct payments remain because only a few authorities have enabled intermediaries to manage personal budgets.

This has meant that the benefits of personal budgets have largely been restricted to those with high levels of competence or those with strong family support.

Personal budgets have now become part of the system, but in a way that has eroded much of their essential role and value. There are no clear entitlements, management costs are disguised and people have little understanding of the flexibility, control or the support that they should receive. Frequently it is the old system, in new clothes.

As *Figure 1* represents, while the innovation was developed through its first two stages it did not really evolve through the third and fourth stages. Instead government, in its hurry to declare success, corrupted the innovation. Largely it became an extension of direct payments (a prior innovation) or a minor amendment to prior commissioning practices. Of course further progress remains possible and work continues to sustain or develop the original thinking. However, the fact that it is now possible for local authorities to claim that they have implemented personal budgets, when in fact they have simply renamed older practices, means that much of the original momentum has been lost.

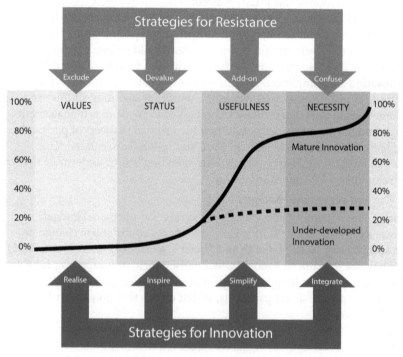

Figure 1. Strategies for Implementing or Reisisting Innovation

Innovation and Government

This is not a story of incompetence. My learning from this experience is not just that government cannot innovate, rather it is that government is most competent at undermining any new idea and defending the system from change. This is not just a feature of government. As the management thinker Robert Townsend once wrote:

It's a poor bureaucrat who can't stall a good idea until even its sponsor is relieved to see it dead and officially buried. [Townsend, 1970, p. 53]

While all bureaucracies may be good at killing innovations, government has some serious advantages. It can use its legal power to effectively steal intellectual property, it can rename things and dictate how ideas are perceived, it can spend ridiculous amounts of money and it can even declare that failure is success. The costs of disagreeing with Government are so high that we are almost impelled to agree to its rewriting of reality! Steve Jobs once said:

"Design is a funny word. Some people think design means how it looks. But of course, if you dig deeper, it's really how it works. The design of the Mac wasn't what it looked like, although that was part of it. Primarily, it was how it worked. To design something really well, you have to get it. You have to really get what it's all about. It takes a passionate commitment to really thoroughly understand something, chew it up, not just quickly swallow it. Most people don't take the time to do that." (Wolf, 1996)

Design and innovation is simply outside the scope of government. Government's ability to ruin an innovation could be thought of as taking a beautiful horse, killing it, turning it into sausages, reassembling a horse from the same sausages and then trying to take the sausage-horse for a ride. Government may recognise something as valuable, but it lacks the integrity – in the literal sense – to understand and develop an innovation.

Final lessons

I think there are at least two important lessons for us to learn from this rather dismal pattern. For social innovators it is perhaps best to try and develop forms of innovation that are as distant as possible from the influence of government. For instance, most of the advantages of personal budgets can be replicated within the form of a support organisation, as we demonstrated at Inclusion Glasgow. Extending personal budgets as a form of support without relying on Government may have been a more effective approach.

There is also an important lesson here in how we think about and try to reform Government itself. One of the most telling features of this story is the way in which the civil service, in particular, preferred to focus on research, implementation or management strategies, as opposed to clear legal reform. This is probably because legal changes are more difficult and demand scrutiny from Parliament. Spending money, commissioning research or overseeing targets is a much safer process for the civil service to oversee.

Perhaps what this implies is that we need to discipline government to avoid the kinds of activities that obscure or delay innovation and to focus its energy only on the strictly legal matters that are the proper function of Government. If we could more clearly distinguish the proper legal architecture of government from its inappropriate managerial tendencies, we may start to see a better balance between administration and innovation. Good law would be careful to avoid over-specifying how a duty should be fulfilled or a right maintained and would leave room for innovation. Legal change would be the role of democratic debate and would be subject to much greater accountability.

In fact, is this not a much more dignified role for the citizen and the community? It is our role to solve problems and develop innovations. As we found with personal budgets, people are much better than systems at making things better for themselves, their families or their communities. The critical error is to expect systems to solve problems that they are not designed to solve.

Citizens need to take more responsibility for solving the problems they can solve themselves, individually or collectively. Citizens also need to recognise when they must organise and demand changes to unjust laws. We must be prepared to advocate for fair distributions of resources and challenge inequality and oppression. We must abandon our orthodox faith in the omni-competence of government, not because government is bad or incompetent, it is not. It just can't do everything well.

Dr Simon Duffy *is the founder and Director of the Centre for Welfare Reform. He is best known for inventing personal budgets and for designing systems of self-directed support*

References

Fitzpatrick, J. (2010) 'Personalised Support: How to provide high quality support to people with complex and challenging needs – learning form Partners for Inclusion'. Sheffield, The Centre for Welfare Reform.

Glasby, J. & Littlechild, R. (2009) *Direct Payments and Personal Budgets – Putting Personalisation into Practice*. The Policy Press.

Health and Social Care Information Centre (2015) 'Community Care Statistics: Social Services Activity, England 2014-15, Final release'. Leeds, Health and Social Care Information Centre.

HM Government (2007) 'Putting People First'. London, HM Government.

Hay, M. & Waters, J. (2009) 'Steering My Own Course'. In Control Publications, London.

Needham, C. and Glasby, J. (eds.) (2014) *Debates in Personalisation*. Policy Press.

O'Brien, J. & Mount, B. (2015) *Pathfinders: people with developmental disabilities and the allies building communities that work work better for everyone*. Inclusion Press.

Pitts, J., Soave, V. and Waters, J. (2009) 'Doing It Your Way: the story of self-directed support in Worcestershire'. London, In Control Publications.

6. Family Intervention doesn't work

Stephen Crossley

What we know works is this thing called family intervention and what it does is basically get into the actual family, in their front room and if actually the kids aren't in school it gets in there and says to the parents I'm gonna show you and explain to you exactly how to get your kids up and out every single day and then I'm gonna make you do it. And if you don't do it, there are gonna be consequences. So it's quite tough, but it's also incredibly caring. And that intense approach works, we know it works because we've already looked at studies that show that this works, basically, and also I've met countless families that have been turned around. (Louise Casey, 2 September 2013)

There is, at the current time, a widespread belief that a number of social ills can be ameliorated or even resolved through state intervention in family life. Politicians, children's charities and social commentators have all suggested that working intensively with families is the right thing to do to tackle issues such as anti-social behaviour (ASB), school exclusion and criminality. When David Cameron was Prime Minister, he went as far as to say, "whatever the social issue we want to grasp – the answer should always begin with family' (Cameron, 2014). A 'family intervention' approach that became popular under the New Labour governments and which sees a keyworker working intensively with 'problem' or 'troubled' families, is being touted as a model that can not only 'tackle' these families, but also help to re-design the way that the state engages with them. The hands-on 'persistent, assertive and challenging' approach of family intervention workers has been contrasted with the putative approach of contemporary social workers and other officials who, in the words of Louise Casey, the senior civil servant in charge of government efforts to tackle 'troubled families', 'circle' (PAC, 2014: 21) and 'assess the hell' out of families' (Ibid: 42) but 'don't actually make any difference' (in Bennett, 2012: 15).

The Troubled Families Programme, established in the aftermath of the 2011 riots, proposed to 'turn around' the lives of the 120,000 most troubled and troublesome families by the end of April 2015 using family intervention approaches. At the launch of the programme, Cameron (2011) stated that he wanted to be clear who he meant when he used the term 'troubled families':

> *Officialdom might call them 'families with multiple disadvantages'.*
> *Some in the press might call them 'neighbours from hell'. Whatever*
> *you call them, we've known for years that a relatively small number of*
> *families are the source of a large proportion of the problems in society.*
> *Drug addiction. Alcohol abuse. Crime. A culture of disruption and*
> *irresponsibility that cascades through generations.*

Troubled families were officially defined as those who

- are involved in crime and anti-social behaviour
- have children not in school
- have an adult on out of work benefits
- cause high costs to the public purse. (DCLG, 2012: 9)

All 152 local authorities in England were involved in the delivery of the programme and the work was funded on a Payment by Results (PbR) basis. Local authorities would be paid an initial attachment fee when they started working with families and would then receive additional funding when they had achieved specific outcomes relating to improved school attendance and reductions in crime or ASB, or an adult moving into continuous employment (see Lowes' chapter in this book on outcome-based commissioning).

Amazingly, in May 2015, the government claimed that it had been 99% successful in turning around these 'troubled families' that had allegedly been causing problems for generations (see Crossley, 2015 for a critique of this claim). A second phase of the TFP is now underway, aimed at turning around 400,000 more 'troubled families' that were identified using different criteria to the original 120,000. The new 'troubled families' are those who also have issues such as health problems, where a child is deemed as being 'in need' and where there exists a risk of financial exclusion. In addition to this expansion, the family intervention approach has been proposed as a way of improving public service delivery in other areas such as child protection cases and adult social care services and public health. In September 2015, Cameron namechecked the success of the TFP when making the case for a 'smarter', more efficient and business-like state, one where 'you could do more with less'. Cameron argued for a state where 'State monopolies should be broken and new providers with great ideas should be welcomed' and where those 'providers should be paid by the results they achieve' (Cameron, 2015).

Heresy

The potential of a triple success in 'turning around' 'troubled families' at the same time as 'turning around' the state, all whilst saving 'the taxpayer' money is undeniably seductive and, to date, little public scrutiny of the claims surrounding the 'family intervention' model has taken place.

But when one scratches the surface of the alluring political rhetoric about dedicated workers, standing side-by-side with disadvantaged families, and being prepared to 'walk in their shoes', one finds that there is little actual evidence that 'family intervention' approaches are capable of 'turning around' the lives of 'troubled families' or addressing the more complex issues that they face. This is not to deny that many families would benefit from someone providing them with practical hands-on support in their domestic work. Indeed, many middle-class families pay for exactly the same kind of domestic help that is supposedly provided through the TFP. But it is hard to see how non-specialist family workers can improve labour market conditions in some of the most deprived areas of the country or, indeed, how they can overcome some of the potential effects of poverty, such as poor physical and mental health and poor educational attainment.

Put simply, 'family intervention' does not have the ability to overcome or even to compensate for the broad effects of structural inequalities. A family living in poverty whose children go to school every day are still living in poverty. A mother who is suffering domestic violence may not view fewer police call-outs for ASB at her house, or her partner finding work, as equating to having her life 'turned around'.

Far from addressing the 'root causes' of society's problems, family intervention approaches serve to paper over the cracks caused by poverty, multiple disadvantage and inequality. The intention is not to 'turn around' the lives of 'troubled families' or to 'empower' them. Instead, the approach aims to 'responsibilisze' the families, encouraging them to see themselves as the sole architects of their circumstances and urging them, under threat of sanctions, to manage those circumstances better, without any meaningful attempt to change the material circumstances of the family for the better. Alas, there is little evidence that family intervention approaches achieve even these modest aims.

Right or wrong?

There is a long history of state intervention in the lives of families it deems to be problematic, but the particular model of family intervention being discussed here has its roots in a charity project in Dundee. The Dundee Families Project worked with families that were purportedly exhibiting anti-social behaviour, and included three different strands: residence in a 'core block' for three or four of the most 'problematic' families; dispersed tenancies; and outreach work. The evaluation of the project (Dillane *et al*, 2001) suggested that 59% of the families who had engaged with the programme achieved 'successful' outcomes and completed the work goals they agreed with practitioners. The core block and dispersed tenancies services achieved better outcomes than the outreach work service.

The alleged success of the model attracted the attention of the UK government which saw the approach as a suitable way of dealing with so-called 'problem families' in England, whose worst excesses hadn't been curbed by social inclusion strategies or existing ASB interventions. In the transition from a Scottish charitable sector project to a UK government intervention, the name of the approach shifted from the initial benign 'Families Project' in Dundee through, upon reaching England, 'Anti-Social Behaviour Intensive Family Support Projects', to 'Family Intervention Projects'. The punitive discursive turn was also accompanied by the introduction of the threat of sanctions for families who refused to engage with the projects. Following the evaluation of six pilot ASB Intensive Family Support Projects, a national network of 53 Family Intervention Projects (FIPs) was announced by the Labour government in 2006 under a new Respect Action Plan. An evaluation of the network of FIPs (Lloyd et al, 2011) has, in turn, been used as justification for the approach that underpins the TFP.

Whilst politicians from across the political spectrum and civil servants have been quick to talk up the success of the family intervention approach, a small number of researchers have cast a more critical eye over some of the claims made on behalf of this 'pioneering' approach. David Gregg (2010), perhaps the most vociferous critic of family intervention projects has argued that government commissioned evaluations of the projects are 'a classic case of policy-based evidence', offering politicians the empirical justification they need to pursue their preferred policy option. Gregg (2010: 2) notes that across three separate evaluations (Dillane et al, 2001; Nixon et al, 2008; White et al, 2008) in both England and Scotland, the evidence suggests that 'FIPs fail in multiple ways':

> ...by targeting the wrong people for the wrong reasons; by targeting false 'causes of ASB' while failing to tackle the real underlying causes in those targeted; by failing to deliver support in key areas like mental health; by failing to deliver sustained changes in family behaviour or reduced ASB in the community.

His analysis of the evaluations highlights a number of issues that cast doubt on the ability of FIPs to 'turn around' the lives of the most troublesome or anti-social families. Gregg notes that a willingness to participate in the projects was part of the selection criteria, suggesting that the most troublesome families might simply refuse to engage. Many of the families entering the projects had low levels of ASB associated with them and many had no police call-outs to their home that related to ASB. This picture did not fit with the 'problem families' rhetoric, and Gregg (2010: 11) argued that criminality rates were 'sexed up' as a result of conflating an individual's involvement of ASB with them being part of a 'problem family'. The researchers involved with the evaluations often identified that it was not possible to determine whether or not changes occurring within families had happened as a direct result of involvement with the FIPs. One evaluation (Nixon *et al*, 2008: 10) also highlighted that

> *Contrary to popular belief, the evidence suggests that rather than constituting a distinct minority distinguishable from the 'law abiding majority', families tended to conform to the norms and values of the communities in which they lived.*

Similar concerns emerge when analysing the last government evaluation on FIPs, which was referenced by David Cameron at the launch of the TFP. This report (Lloyd *et al*, 2011) highlights that there was, 'on average, a 50 per cent reduction in the proportion of families involved in crime and ASB' (2011: 4), and only around 40 per cent saw improvements in mental health and 20% entered employment (Lloyd *et al*, 2011: 1-2). The sustainability of these outcomes was difficult to ascertain and those families who were not followed up after leaving the FIPs were the ones who achieved less positive outcomes. Finally, the report (2011: 7) states that whilst the study 'provides clear evidence that FIPs reduce crime and ASB amongst the families they work with', there is 'limited evidence that FIPs generate better outcomes than other non-FIP interventions on family functioning or health issues'.

When a similar level of scrutiny is applied to claims of 'success' in turning around the most 'troubled families under the TFP, the claims unravel just as quickly. When the government published a report entitled Understanding Troubled Families (DCLG, 2014), drawing on information about families participating in the TFP, it was argued that the problems experienced and caused by the families were more severe than initially thought. The report stated that families, on average, experienced 9 different problems on entry to the programme and Casey referred to them as the 'worst families in Britain' who 'cause the most problems' (quoted in Little, 2014). Although the data, collected by local authority practitioners and using different methods, is not particularly robust, a different reading of the information on families suggests that the families did not fit the 'neighbours from hell' stereotype that the government sought to attach to them.

For example, far from being involved with high levels of crime and ASB, the data (collected from around 8,400 families who entered the programme in its early stages) suggested that, in many families, there were often only individuals who were involved in very low levels of crime or ASB (Crossley, 2015: 5). This is demonstrated by the figures below:

- 85% of families had no adults with a proven criminal offence in the previous 6 months
- 97% of families had children with either one or no criminal offences in the previous 6 months
- 58% of families had no police callouts in the previous 6 months

- 95% of families had no family members identified as being Prolific and Priority Offenders (PPO)
- 89% of families had no adult subject to an ASB intervention

Similarly, the majority of families who lived in rented housing were paying their rent on time, weren't in arrears and weren't under threat of eviction for any reason. Only 7% of families had members who had been clinically diagnosed as being dependent on alcohol and the same percentage had members who had been diagnosed as being addicted to non-prescription drugs. Around three-quarters of all of the families had no young people classed as being 'Not in Education, Employment or Training' (NEET) on entry to the programme and a higher number of families (84%) had children who hadn't been permanently excluded from school. Around a quarter of the families actually had an adult member in work on entry into the programme (see also Crossley, 2014). Separate data collected on the reason the employment situation of 'troubled families' highlighted that only around one-third of the 'out-of-work' families involved in the programme were actually in a position to seek work. The reminder had family members on Incapacity benefit, Employment Support Allowance, Income Support or Carers Allowance, which are paid to people who are generally considered to be unable to work, for a variety of reasons (DWP, 2015).

This may help to explain how, despite the government claiming that local authorities had turned around the lives of 99% of the 'troubled families' they worked with under Phase 1, only around 10% of these families had seen an adult member move off out-of-work benefits. Around 8000 families, which government claimed had been 'turned around' as a result of the family intervention they had received via the TFP, were actually turned around by data matching exercises, where local authorities used available crime and community safety, education and employment data to claim success for families who 'turned themselves around', without any 'family intervention' at all (Bawden, 2015).

What needs to change?

> '... my mission in politics – the thing I am really passionate about – is fixing the responsibility deficit.' (David Cameron, 15 December 2011, launch of the Troubled Families Programme)

The problems with promoting 'family intervention' as the answer to disadvantaged families troubles do not just revolve around a lack of substantive evidence with which to promote the idea that it 'works'. There is a much larger body of work, the fruits of around a century's worth of social scientific enquiry, which highlights structural and societal, rather than familial, roots to disadvantage and deviancy.

If David Cameron was serious when he argued that his real passion in politics is 'fixing the responsibility deficit' and 'building a stronger society', as he did at the launch of the TFP, he would do well to start by taking a look at the state's abdication of its responsibilities towards its citizens. We have an education system that consistently fails working-class children and a higher education system that offers diminishing returns on an investment of around £9000 per annum on tuition fees alone. The well-known social determinants of health are marginalised in government policies which prefer 'nudging' people towards making better 'lifestyle choices' over more expansive forms of state action to counter the detrimental effects of inequality on people's health.

If the government wanted to take responsibility for these issues, they could. A stigmatising system of 'welfare' that increasingly sees poor people, rather than poverty, as the problem to be solved, could be replaced by a comprehensive system of 'social security' that enabled people who relied on it to achieve an adequate standard of living. Drug and alcohol addictions and their related issues could be viewed as problems that require supportive health services rather than punitive criminal justice enforcement measures. A universal system of family support could undoubtedly help many families, if other factors such as housing affordability and labour market conditions were also being addressed at the same time. But when 'family intervention' is advanced as the only game in town, at the same time that universal services are being cut and families are being made poorer by welfare reforms, it amounts to nothing less than a temporary sticking plaster for societies gaping wounds. Powerful symbolic and material change is necessary, and possible. We cannot continue to individualise or familialise the social problems that poverty and inequality create.

Stephen Crossley, is a Senior Lecturer in Social Policy at Northumbria University

References

Bawden, A. (2015) Is the success of the government's troubled families scheme too good to be true? *The Guardian*, 11 November , http://www.theguardian.com/society/2015/nov/11/troubled-family-programme-government-success-council-figures

Bennett, R. (2012) Local Authority Officials 'should scrub floors', *The Times*, 27 April, p15

Cameron, D. (2011) Troubled families speech, 15 December, https://www.gov.uk/government/speeches/troubled-families-speech

Cameron, D., (2014) Speech at the Relationships Alliance Summit, 18 August, https://www.gov.uk/government/speeches/david-cameron-on-families

Cameron, D. (2015) Prime Minister: My vision for a smarter state, 11 September, https://www.gov.uk/government/speeches/prime-minister-my-vision-for-a-smarter-state

Casey, L. (2013) Former Portsmouth police officer back on Asbo beat, BBC Online, 2 September. http://www.bbc.co.uk/news/uk-england-hampshire-23896776

Crossley, S. (2014) '(Mis)Understanding 'troubled families" https://akindoftrouble.files.wordpress.com/2014/10/misunderstanding-troubled-families-working-paper-v2.pdf

Crossley, S. (2015) 'The Troubled Families Programme: the perfect social policy?' Centre for Crime and Justice Studies, Briefing 13. http://www.crimeandjustice.org.uk/sites/crimeandjustice.org.uk/files/The%20Troubled%20Families%20Programme%2C%20Nov%202015.pdf

DCLG (2012) 'Working with Troubled Families', Department for Communities and Local Government

DCLG (2014) 'Understanding Troubled Families', Department for Communities and Local Government

DWP (2015) 'Troubled Families Experimental Official Statistics - July 2015', Department for Work and Pensions. https://www.gov.uk/government/uploads/system/uploads/attachment_data/file/464159/troubled-families-experimental-official-stats-july-2015.pdf

Dillane, J., Hill, M., Bannister, J., Scott, S. (2001), 'Evaluation of The Dundee Family Project', Centre for the Child & Society and Department of Urban Studies, University of Glasgow. www.scotland.gov.uk/Resource/Doc/158814/0043122.pdf

Gregg, D. (2010) 'Family intervention projects: a classic case of policy-based evidence,' Centre for Crime and Justice Studies. http://www.crimeandjustice.org.uk/sites/crimeandjustice.org.uk/files/family%20intervention.pdf

Little, A. (2014) 'Welfare squads to target problem families costing UK £30bn', Daily Express, 18 August, p1

Lloyd, C., Wollny, I., White, C., Gowland, S. & Purdon, S. (2011) 'Monitoring and evaluation of family intervention services and projects between February 2007 and March 201, Department for Education. https://www.gov.uk/government/uploads/system/uploads/attachment_data/file/184031/DFE-RR174.pdf

Nixon, J., Parr, S., Hunter, C., Sanderson, D. & Whittle, S. (2008) 'The longer term outcomes for families who had worked with Intensive Family Support Projects', Department for Communities and Local Government. www.communities.gov.uk/documents/housing/doc/familysupportprojects.doc

PAC (2014) Uncorrected transcript of oral evidence, Programme to help families facing multiple challenges, Public Accounts Committee, 29 January. http://www.parliament.uk/documents/commons-committees/public-accounts/PAC-290114.pdf

White, C., Warrener, M., Reeves, A., La Valle, I. (2008), 'Family Intervention Projects: An Evaluation of Their Design, Setup and Early Outcomes'; National Centre for Social Research, DCSF-RW047. www.dcsf.gov.uk/research/data/uploadfiles/acf44f.pdf

7. Full of Sound and Fury: Biology meets Policy

Sue White and Dave Wastell

There is a settled assumption that with increasing technological advances the State will be able to intervene to prevent a range of social ills in new, efficient and cost-effective ways. Full of good intentions, the prevention paradigm reigns. This chapter makes the case against the aspiration to 'fix' people.

Some might presume that research aimed at understanding the intersection of biology and social environment is 'blue skies' and therefore very much in the academic realm. In practice, ideas and discoveries presented by biomedical science are often particularly compelling. Providers of services not only want good evidence to justify difficult decisions they have to make; they are also susceptible as anyone to the persuasive nature of hard scientific 'facts' (Early Intervention Foundation, Feb 2016).

The pronouncements of leading biotechnoscientists are listened to with respect previously given only to the most eminent of nuclear physicists; today they advise government and industry, and give well-received lectures to the world leaders at Davos. (Rose and Rose, 2012: 277)

Biological sciences, particularly neuroscience and genomics, are currently in the ascent. These new "techno-sciences" increasingly promise to provide a theory of everything in the natural and social worlds. Social policy has not been slow to conscript technological biology. Beginning with the decade of the brain in the USA in the 1990s, neuroscience was first onto the stage, but developments in genomics, known as epigenetics, also have implications for society and culture and the responses of the State to intimate family life and personal choices. In this brief essay, we examine the actual and potential applications of contemporary biology in social policy, and their implications for moral debate and state intervention. These are addressed in greater detail in Wastell and White (forthcoming).

The insurgence of evolutionary biology and neuropsychology have been spurred by technological innovations such as brain imaging and molecular genetics. The 'neuro' prefix, as we shall see, is now applied to disciplines as disparate as economics, the law, aesthetics, pedagogy, theology and organizational behaviour. The term 'neuromania' has been coined (Legrenzi and Umilta, 2011; Tallis, 2011) to refer to this proliferation. Although some critics have lampooned this ebullience, speaking flippantly of parts of the brain 'lighting up' in overly-simplistic laboratory experiments, there are many, very real implications in seeing the human condition in this way. Social Policy is making increasingly significant use of neuroscientific evidence to warrant particular claims about both the soaring potentialities and irreversible vulnerabilities of early childhood and the proper responses of the State. Neuroscience is also making its mark in the area of criminal justice, where it often appears to offer 'liberalizing' benefits: developmental neuroscience has been used, for example, to make the case for raising the age of criminal responsibility. However, alongside these apparently progressive arguments lies, for example, the seductive (and perhaps sinister) idea that violent crime can be attributed to a small group of intrinsically aggressive individuals, and that neuroimaging (or genetics) can yield 'biomarkers' which may be used to identify risky people and to 'target' interventions. This prefigures a dystopian future in which new biological technologies play an increasing role in pre-emptively isolating 'dangerous' subgroups and identifying how to prevent their predicted deviance.

Moralising the Stuff of Life

The last decades have thus seen a profound shift in our understanding of biological processes and life itself. At the heart of neurobiology's ascendancy is a paradox, described by Rose and Rose thus:

> [Biological] discourses are at once essentialist and Promethean; they see human nature as fixed, while at the same time offering to transform human life through the real and imagined power of the biotechnosciences. (2012: 24)

Whereas genetics has conventionally focused on examining the DNA sequence (the genotype), the burgeoning field of epigenetics examines additional mechanisms for modifying gene expression in manifest behaviours, traits, physical features, health status and so on (the phenotype). It provides a conduit mediating the interaction of the environment on an otherwise immutable DNA blueprint, and invites a natural interest in the impact of adverse conditions, such as deprivation or normatively deficient parenting. The implications of this new "biology of social adversity" (Boyce *et al.*, 2012) for social policy are far reaching. 'Hard' heredity, in which genes were seen as inherited and fixed for life (insulated from environmental influences, life chances and choices) drove the eugenics movement of the late nineteenth and early twentieth century. In its extreme form, the 'barbarous utopia' of the Nazis (Meloni, 2016: 28) severed biology from the acceptable face of politics and social engineering. Epigenetics shows every sign of rendering biology political and moral again. As Meloni notes, freeing us from the determinacy of our genetic inheritance might help make the case for more resources to 'fix' or prevent damage to the epigenome of disadvantaged groups, but it may also have less desirable sequelae:

This all sounds desirable, but how likely is it in a society where class,
race, and gender inequalities remain so vast? What is our society
going to make of the notion that... the socially disadvantaged are
also (epi)genetically damaged? ... And what will oppressed groups do
with this flurry of epigenetic studies concerning their own condition?
(Meloni 2016: 221)

Political positions are already emerging. The slavery reparations
movement in the United States is using epigenetic arguments to support
its case for compensation for the privations of slavery generations
ago (Tribune242, 2015) and there are also claims that the offspring of
Holocaust survivors show enduring epigenetic changes (Meloni, 2016).
Legal scholars and ethicists are further commenting on the implications
for litigation in relation to the effects of a range of environmental and
workplace toxins:

[I]nsurance policy claims and tort liability may have a "long tail"
if the toxic effects from agents acting via an epigenetic mechanism
are not manifested until one or more generations into the future.
(Rothstein *et al*, 2009: 11)

The efflorescence of technobiology brings with it a welter of complex
moral issues and internal contradictions. On the one hand, it can be
seen as a 'giant leap' in the ever-ascending modernist project of human
progress, but even within medicine, where epigenetically-based drug
treatments have real promise and are beginning to appear, and where
the moral arguments for their use are less contentious, the science is as
yet unsettled. In fixing one thing we may very easily finish up breaking
another. For example, epigenetic arguments potentially engender newly
racialised and stigmatised identities consequent on epigenetic 'damage',
and the moral imperative to 'optimise' the uterine environment in
particular (Mansfield and Guthman, 2014). These may be resisted by
those very disadvantaged groups who have come under the epigenetic
gaze. The following online comment from a Glaswegian citizen following
publication in the press of the results of a study of the inhabitants of his
city is an illustration of how the stories may be received, and resisted:

"I am just flabbergasted by this latest research – I am 81 years old
and was born into what I would describe as extreme poverty ... but
with caring parents who were not into accepting 'charity' but gave me
and my siblings the best they could in spite of a lot of unemployment.
I have led a useful life, was pretty intelligent at school, and held
responsible jobs, have married successfully, had children ... and feel
I was anything but deprived or damaged. Just grateful that these
statistics weren't available in my past!"
(Citied in Meloni, 2016: 221)

If gene expression is adaptive, it can be changed for the better or worse at the molecular level. Once the genome is rewritten as malleable, and vulnerable to lifestyle and patterns of nurture, this is likely to create newly moralised domains and concomitant responsibilities. What implications are likely to ensue, we may ask, of a moral imperative that requires each generation to maintain the quality of the human genome and epigenome and pass it on in no worse condition than the present generation received it? How does it change your relationship with your mother, for example, if you see yourself not as the latest in a line of anxious people, part of a family of worriers, and instead as an epigenetically compromised individual, damaged in utero, or in early childhood by your 'neurotic' or distracted mother?

Addressing cancer at the molecular level has an intuitive rightness about it, provided the epigenetic mechanism can be identified and properly targeted. However, even in this domain, safe, effective treatments have proved rather elusive. For example, whilst there have been successes with blood cancers, the troublesome habit of epigenetic drugs affecting all cells, not just cancer cells, means they can prove highly toxic. Nevertheless one can see a clear link from the molecular science to a possible pharmacological treatment for a wholly unpleasant disease. The molecular level might equally further our understandings of the impacts of toxins or infectious agents. Things become much more murky when policy is focused on behavioural changes on the precautionary principle that a variety of quite ordinary 'choices' might be damaging the epigenome for the next and even subsequent generations.

What to do with the Recalcitrant Few?

Significantly absent from many of the otherwise sophisticated discussions about the potential uses of epigenetic understandings is the proper response of the state to those who refuse to comply with actions deemed to be in their own best interests, or in the interests of their future offspring. Yet, these are thorny matters indeed as Rothstein *et al* (2009) note:

> [E]pigenetics raises difficult questions about the obligations of society
> to preserve the soundness of the human genome and epigenome
> for the benefit of future generations. In developing a principle of
> intergenerational equity for the human genome and epigenome,
> optimum social policy lies between indifference to the health burdens
> of future generations and eugenic notions of manipulating heredity to
> improve the human condition. (p.27)

It is important to note that current developments in biotechnology are not historically unique; arguably they form part of an enduring project to 'fix' people which has, in its various guises, both liberal and conservative valences, but which tends to lead policy and professional reasoning in particular directions. Prevention and targeting are prominent motifs in an increasingly residual and conditional welfare settlement, providing a natural slot for technologies which can claim to tease out individual susceptibilities. Rather than challenging orthodoxies, both neuroscience and epigenetics at present appear to be being used to support old moral arguments, regardless of what the scientists might anticipate amongst themselves. As Kahn (2009: 311) notes:

> [S]cience is not an anthropomorphic being, it does not 'tell' anything. Scientific data has no meaning until one interprets it and such interpretations are inevitably packed with qualitative judgements.

At present the moral mood music seems to take us into the inhospitable womb. Studies on 'foetal programming' by adverse 'maternal mood' burgeon, drawing much inspiration from laboratory work on rats. An initial trawl on Google Scholar yields 30,000 hits for foetal programming. This is a field of frenetic scientific activity. Given the range of environments in which human beings have thrived for millennia, we must ask ourselves why the preoccupation with stress in utero, where the infant not the mother is the focus of expert concern, and where does this activity lead us as a society?

Epigenetic thinking is Janus faced, as Mansfield and Guthman (2014) note. It breaks out of the straitjacket of genetic determinism – we are molecularly free. We are porous, we absorb, we interact. These understandings may inform fights for social justice, add a punch to arguments for compensation following exposure to environmental chemicals, show how oppression gets under the skin. But all this plasticity has a dark side:

> This ugly side of epigenetics arises out of the heart of what makes epigenetics promising: that it focuses on plasticity, rather than determinism... makes it open to intervention and improvement, even 'optimization' ... [but] The notion of optimization renders epigenetic changes as disorderly, as damage not adaptation.... things once normal, in a statistical sense, can become abnormal, in the sense of not-optimal'. (p.3 and p.11)

Gestation becomes the playground for epigenetic manipulations. Women are responsible for optimising good biological influences, making the right choices' consuming the remedies and therapies on offer to 'optimise' their uterine environments. We thus come perilously close to losing the category 'normal'. It is squeezed and squeezed until the molecules squeal. This is a paradox because epigenetics is about difference and inevitable variation in response to the outside world, but by equating difference with disease through the notion of suboptimal conditions it creates a particularly potent form of eugenic thinking. In the USA this is heavily racialised as Mansfield and Guthman note. This side of the Atlantic this modus operandi is almost certainly going to be valanced through social class.

'Optimisation' of early life environments and the conflation of 'suboptimal' with 'marginal maltreatment' might make the case for benignly intended public health and parenting education approaches (Barlow and Calam 2011), but they also erode the 'normal' and expose particular sections of the population to increased scrutiny in the name of prevention. The State has new mandates to screen and intervene to prevent what might have been. We can see harbingers of what might be on the way. There are epidemiological studies linking fathers' lifestyle (smoking, diet) to disease risk in the male line (Pembrey, et al., 2006), and arguments from developmental biologists in favour of broad ranging public health or environmental interventions.

> [T]here is compelling evidence that the male germline is also vulnerable to environmental impacts which confer substantial health risks on offspring. The clear implication of these findings is that effective mitigation of environmental health risks is unlikely to be achieved by sex, or life-stage-specific behavior change, but will require action that recognizes the much greater breadth of these risks across the life course. (Cunliffe 2015:67)

Nevertheless, developments in the policy world support Mansfield and Guthman's arguments. It is mothers who will bear the brunt of the current epigenetic line of reasoning.

Biologically uniting nature and nurture, epigenetics promises a great deal and is delivering crucial new understandings of disease, but it also reconfigures relationships between parents, children and the state. The difficulties in accessing biological samples from the brains of human subjects has led to a search for reliable markers in peripheral tissues as proxies for changes to the central nervous system. A current favourite is cheek (buccal) cells. The relatively uninvasive nature of such tests opens up the population to epigenetic screening. As well as parent reports and teacher assessments, a recent protocol for the evaluation of an early intervention project by the 'Warwick Consortium' (2014) includes: *a number of biometric measures (e.g. hair samples to assess cortisol levels at 2 years; buccal cheek swabs to assess epigenetic changes at 3 years; accelerometers to assess activity at 7 years.* (page 4)

A Road Map to Hell ....

In 2015, Adam Perkins a neurobiologist of personality wrote *The Welfare Trait: How State Benefits Affect Personality*. The book's central argument is encapsulated below:

> Childhood disadvantage has been shown in randomised controlled experiments – the gold standard of scientific proof – to promote the formation of an aggressive, antisocial and rule breaking personality profile that impairs occupational and social adjustment during adulthood...A welfare state that increases the number of children born into disadvantaged households therefore risks increasing the number of citizens who develop an aggressive, antisocial and rule-breaking personality profile due to being exposed to disadvantage during childhood (p2-3)

Perkins' road is paved with good intentions: preserving the welfare state for the worthy by ridding it of the burden of the employment resistant personality type. Perkins' reasoning is biological. He reductively attributes the perverse incentives (to avoid work) potentially inherent in welfare regimes, to a biologically and neurologically programmed personality type: the 'employment resistant personality'. The claims, evoking animal models, are bold:

Selective breeding for personality causes significant genetically influenced changes in personality within as few as five generations. As a caveat, these experiments present extreme examples. It should be noted that there is more variation in human mating than in selective breeding studies of the type cited here, so the rate of change in human personality due to welfare-related selective breeding will be slower (p111).

A moral project thus manifests itself on a number of levels from the individualised intervention to the opaque models of the macro-economists which aim to inform social policy. The consequences of the current dominant moral and scientific settlements are that preferred policy responses are individualised and increasingly medicalised. A preoccupation with prevention, early intervention and particular forms of evidence are squeezing out conversations about different and potentially more desirable and sustainable actions to make people's lives better.

Conclusion: Looking in the Wrong Places

Are the neurological and molecular levels, the actions and processes within and between cells, necessarily the most rich and appropriate to guide the actions of the State. They resolutely lead us in the direction of fixing people, not helping them to keep going, or building communities or indeed alleviating poverty. But we must ask, are people actually broken? Normality itself is a disappearing category, with more and more of the ups and downs of life, its stresses, sorrows and disappointments coming within the psychiatric "gaze". The idea that there is "one normal", rather than many, is the fundamental problem. Inevitably, this leads to a progressive shrinkage of the membership of the category "normal", as the exclusion principle operates, eventually to zero, or at least potentially to a very exclusive elite

Attempts to fathom the depths of life by examining our flesh and blood create new imperatives for the state. Here in the moral domains of deviance, normality, crime, punishment, the making of socially useful human capital can be turned into technical matters to be sorted and shaped. Prevention and surveillance go under the skin and into the womb. Questions about what is expectable of parents, what are acceptable levels of care for children, and crucially the limits of freedom and what the State can meaningfully and ethically offer and who may profit, are surely moral ones and need informed, open debate. Yet, biological forms of reasoning are likely to result in greater opportunities for big pharma and possibly fewer for social housing projects and food cooperatives which have little currency at the molecular level and often struggle to demonstrate the sort of 'outcomes' economists prefer to plug into their models aimed at the optimisation of 'human capital'. It is easier in the short term to show the effects of a pill on a biomarker than of access to decent food and some human company on the wellbeing on a community – especially if nobody gets a job as a result. Is this what we want for our children?

Sue White, Professor of Social Work, Department of Sociological Studies at Sheffield University

David Wastell, Emeritus Professor, Nottingham University Business School

References

Barlow, J., Calam, R. (2011). A public health approach to safeguarding in the 21st century. *Child Abuse Review*, 20(4), 238-255.

Boyce, W. T., Sokolowski, M. B., & Robinson, G. E. (2012). Toward a new biology of social adversity. *Proceedings of the National Academy of Sciences*, 109 (Supplement 2), 17143-17148

Cunliffe, V. (2015) Experience-sensitive epigenetic mechanisms, developmental plasticity, and the biological embedding of chronic disease risk. *WIREs Syst. Biol. Med.* 2015, 7:53–71.

Early Intervention Foundation (2016) Call for submission: 'What is known about interactions between biology and the social environment in relation to early intervention and prevention?' http://www.eif.org.uk/call-for-submission-what-is-known-about-interactions-between-biology-and-the-social-environment-in-relation-to-early-intervention-and-prevention/

Khan, F. (2010). 'Preserving human potential as freedom: a framework for regulating epigenetic harms'. *Health Matrix*, 20, 259.

Legrenzi, P., Umilta, C. (2011) *Neuromania: on the limits of brain science.* Oxford University Press

Mansfield, B., Guthman, J. (2014). 'Epigenetic life: biological plasticity, abnormality, and new configurations of race and reproduction.' *cultural geographies*, 1474474014555659.

Meloni, M. (2016) *Political Biology Science and Social Values in Human Heredity from Eugenics to Epigenetics.* (ebook) Palgrave.

Pembrey, ME., Bygren, LO., Kaati G., Advinsson S., Northstone, K., Sjostrom M., Golding J. (2006). Sex-specific, male-line transgenerational responses in humans. *European Journal of Human Genetics*, 14, 159-164.

Perkins, A. (2015). *The Welfare Trait: How State Benefits Affect Personality.* Palgrave MacMillan.

Rose, H., Rose, S. (2012) *Genes, Cells and Brains: The Promethean Promises of the New Biology.* London: Verso

Rothstein, M. A., Cai, Y., & Marchant, G. E. (2009). The ghost in our genes: legal and ethical implications of epigenetics. Health Matrix (Cleveland, Ohio: 1991), 19(1), 1.

Tallis, R. (2011) *Aping mankind: Neuromania, darwinitis and the misrepresentation of humanity.* Acumen.

Wastell, D.,White S. (forthcoming 2016 – working title) *Brains, Genes and Magic: Fixing Folk for a Better World*, Policy Press

8. The Performance Management Emperor Has No Clothes

Simon Guilfoyle

Over the last thirty years, UK police performance management has been characterised by a top down command-and-control ethos, along with heavy reliance on simplistic indicators and proxy measures.[1] Coupled with the dominance of numerical targets, league tables and binary comparisons (i.e. comparing a numeric value with a single previous data point, such as 'the same period last year'), this performance culture has become entrenched.

Some forces have started to move away from these practices, but they are still prevalent in many areas.[2] There remains a degree of resistance to change and an unwillingness to challenge what has become a well-established orthodoxy in police performance management, despite the widespread evidence that numerical targets and league tables cause dysfunctional behaviour.

In this chapter I explore what I term the 'three pillars' of traditional police performance management, pointing towards inherent limitations and entirely predictable unintended consequences; furthermore, I assert that these approaches are fundamentally illegitimate and therefore have no place in police performance management systems, or anywhere else.

My heresy is that the UK police service routinely uses meaningless and counterproductive forms of performance information (I anticipate this is mirrored in the wider public and private sectors). This chapter will explain why well-intentioned managers have been doing the wrong things for so long, what can be done instead, and who can make the necessary changes.

Binary Comparisons

The first of the 'three pillars' of traditional police performance management is the use of binary comparisons. The practice involves comparing two isolated numeric values, and interpreting the difference between them as though it were a trend or trajectory. The following statement is typical:

> In April 2014 the number of priority crimes committed fell to 26,297 offences, down 10% from last month and down 11% from the same month last year. Tramlink saw the largest fall (down 23%)... The rate of victims who felt they were treated fairly by the police rose to 91% (up 3%) whilst victim satisfaction rose to 80% (up 4%).
>
> (Greater London Authority, 2014)[3]

Binary comparisons are utterly meaningless because, by definition, the data have no context. When a comparison is made between today's value and another from last week, last month, last year, the same period last year, year-to-date, an average, and so on, it ignores naturally-occurring fluctuations and produces extremely unstable results.

Binary comparisons tend to be used because of their simplicity: and they appear to depict a 'direction of travel' (often emphasised by red and green 'up' and 'down' arrows). The problem is, however, that they are too simplistic. Bird *et al* (2005) of the Royal Statistical Society warns:

> *Very particularly the practice of concentrating on a comparison with the most recent value, this year's results compared with last year's, may be very misleading for reasons including regression to the mean.*
>
> (2005, p.14)[4]

To illustrate the misleading nature of binary comparisons, if one were plotted on a chart, it would look like this:[5]

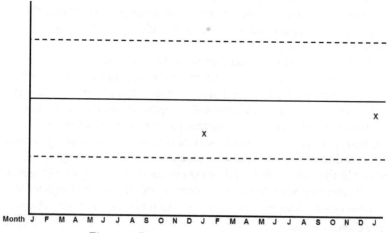

Figure 1. Binary comparison chart

Displaying a binary comparison visually shows how inadequate it is – users are unable to tell if there is indeed a trend over time, or whether either of the values is particularly high or low, part of a pattern, or otherwise of interest. Furthermore, there is nothing to indicate where the parameters of an expected range would be or if the data points would fall within them. The huge empty spaces act as a stark warning that it would be foolish to make any assumptions about the data. But, surprisingly, some managers seem content to accept a narrative such as; Crime is 6.5% higher than it was during the same period last year" without question.

Although it may be possible to compare two sets of numbers using statistical methods that test for significant differences, this is relatively rare in practice. Instead, isolated numeric values are presented alongside simplistic percentage 'differences', often in performance documents filled with multi-coloured numeric tables showing 'month vs month' or 'year vs year' comparisons. This routinely triggers a thoughtless series of events, whereby users first perceive a trajectory ('improving'/'deteriorating', etc.), hypothesise about what may have caused it, then start asking questions, moving resources, writing plans, convening extra meetings, changing tactics and so on – all in the hope that these actions will address the perceived problem.

Despite these good intentions, it may well be the case that the perceived problem does not exist. It could be just normal statistical variation, thereby rendering all those additional meetings and plans redundant. Worse still, whilst attention was focused on a non-existent problem, a genuine issue elsewhere was probably being overlooked.

I find these patterns of behaviour very depressing. They are regularly observed in real-life police performance settings, but have also been verified during a series of psychometric micro-experiments deployed as part of my ongoing PhD research[6] – the study identified that almost 90% of a representative group of police-officer-respondents misinterpreted an experimental binary comparison stimulus in the expected direction (i.e. by assuming it reflected deterioration); they then enacted unwarranted and disproportionate behavioural responses as a direct consequence. These findings were confirmed, with high levels of statistical significance and predictability, and were published as a research paper in a peer-reviewed journal.[7]

In summary, binary comparisons are ill-judged, misleading and fundamentally unhelpful; they aren't valid starting points for asking questions.

An Alternative to Binary Comparisons

One alternative is simply to put the missing numbers back into that chart and look at the data in context. This can be done through the use of Statistical Process Control (SPC).[8] SPC is one method for providing a window into the world of data; it is not a panacea, but it does enable users to see what is actually happening at a glance.

Here is an example of a SPC chart. (The axes aren't labelled, so you can envisage whether the chart relates to crime data, response times, or anything else you particularly care about, at intervals of your choice.) It is immediately apparent that just one data point is significant – and it is the only valid starting point for asking questions here.

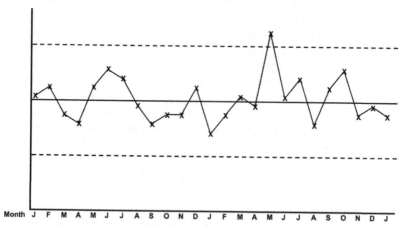

Figure 2. SPC chart

Without going into the detail of how SPC charts are constructed, suffice to say that they are a lot more rigorous than binary comparisons. The boundaries of what is 'normal' are determined by the data themselves, which is usually confirmed with 95% or 99% confidence, depending on the type of chart. Outliers, patterns, trends and trajectories are easily identifiable, meaning that users can focus on areas of genuine concern, rather than have a knee-jerk reaction to random (and minor) fluctuations.

What's more, the same study that confirmed the link between binary comparisons and adverse behavioural responses also found that the same respondents reacted in a more measured fashion when confronted with crime data presented in SPC format.[9]

So there you go – a simple, straightforward and infinitely more powerful alternative to binary comparisons. Seriously, what's not to like?

League Tables

The second 'pillar' of traditional police performance management is the use of league tables. These are used in the healthcare and education sectors, and are commonly used within policing to rank peer groups, thereby inducing assumptions about relative performance. These assumptions then invite praise, criticism, sanction or reward, based on relative positions in the table.

Although the notion of understanding comparative peer performance can be useful for identifying opportunities to learn and improve, attempting to do so through the use of league tables is problematic; they are methodologically unsound and often totally misleading. The main issues are:

1. League tables convey information in a format that is largely meaningless but it triggers unwarranted assumptions about relative performance.
2. These assumptions predictably drive dysfunctional behaviour.

Let's look at these points in turn. First, as a format for presenting data, league tables are over-simplistic and prone to misinterpretation. Wild fluctuations are common and therefore work units swap positions regularly. As with binary comparisons, this is largely due to normal variation; other statistical considerations such as sample sizes, confidence intervals, overlaps and margins of error are also relevant.[10] If these factors are ignored or go unreported then it is inappropriate to ascribe meaning to any apparent 'differences'. Therefore, there is absolutely no basis for attempting to rank the work units concerned.

To illustrate the point regarding confidence intervals and overlaps, consider the diagram below.

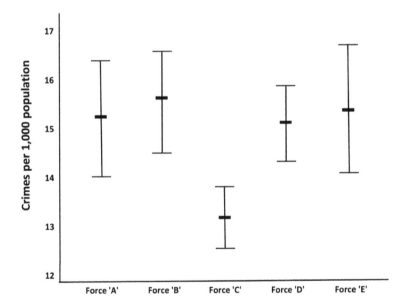

Figure 3. Peer comparisons with confidence intervals

Here it can be seen that all forces except Force 'C' exhibit overlapping confidence intervals and the mean average of each data set (the thick bar in the middle of each line) also falls within the other forces' boundaries. This means we can only say that Force 'C' is significantly different to the other four; it is impossible and inappropriate to rank the other forces.

Conversely, league tables appear to neatly rank from 'top' to 'bottom', yet if there's no information about confidence intervals it's impossible to know if any of the data involve large 'overlaps'. If this vital information is missing, one cannot separate work units from each other to build a league table. Let's face it – about half of those in a league table are 'below average' and someone is always bottom. This occurs regardless of how tightly clustered the work units are, or how well the whole group is performing.

Therefore, only if a genuine trend emerges, or a work unit is significantly different from others in the group, should an attempt be made to understand difference. Otherwise, methodological limitations associated with the construction of neatly-ranked league tables mean they tend to present a false picture and are unsuitable as a means of assessing relative performance.[11] Fundamentally, Goldstein and Spiegelhalter of the Royal Statistical Society contend, '...*current official support for output league tables, even adjusted, is misplaced...*' (1996:405)

The second major issue with league tables is that they drive unnecessary and often downright dysfunctional behaviour; managers demand explanations for 'poor' performance, berate those who appear to be failing, and so on. People then focus on moving up the league table, often engaging in gaming and cheating to do so. There's a wealth of evidence that this happens in healthcare, education, policing and beyond.[12]

An Alternative to League Tables

A better way of assessing comparative peer performance could involve adopting similar principles to those that apply to SPC charts. This is illustrated by the two diagrams below. In configuration 'A', although the six police forces are apparently performing at slightly different levels, they are all within the bounds of what is statistically 'normal' for that group. In configuration 'B', they are displayed in the same order, except that one force is significantly different from the peer group – this provides a mandate to explore potential reasons for this anomaly.

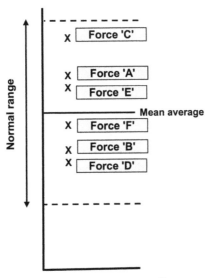

Figure 4. Peer Comparisons: Configuration 'A'

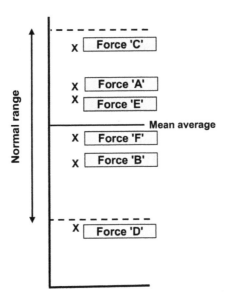

Figure 5. Peer Comparisons: Configuration 'B'

Although the diagrams are intentionally simplified, I hope they help demonstrate the importance of being able to identify whether differences are significant.

Again, during my ongoing PhD research I have used experimental psychometrics to test the predictability of disproportionate or unwarranted behavioural responses being enacted as a consequence of league table use; the results confirmed that where respondents assumed performance was poor, such adverse reactions were indeed highly predictable.

So the well-worn claim, "League tables aren't the problem – it's the way they're used" doesn't cut it for me. Yes, aggressive application is likely to exacerbate dysfunction, but there's something innately illegitimate about the format itself that makes adverse behavioural responses highly likely.[11] Rejecting league tables isn't a case of throwing the baby out with the bathwater, because there is no baby in this bathwater. Instead, simply utilise contextualised diagrams and adhere to well-established statistical principles if you wish to identify significant differences between similar work units. It's irresponsible not to.

Numerical Targets

Numerical targets have been a mainstay of UK police and public sector performance management, gaining impetus and notoriety throughout the 1990s and early 2000s, before appearing to fall out of favour with many politicians and senior officers over the last few years.[13] However, the use of targets persists to this day because managers still believe they are effective and seem oblivious to the well-documented adverse effects.

We will explore these considerations shortly, but first we need to agree on what we mean by the words that we use when we write or talk about numerical targets and associated concepts. Sometimes people read my blog[14] or hear me speak and think I'm against performance management or measurement as a whole – I'm not. I do, however, have a specific concern about the use of numerical targets. You see, 'numerical targets', 'measures' and 'priorities' are three different things, but the words and concepts are often conflated.

Priorities are essential, because activity needs to be focused on the right things. When there is clarity of purpose, defining priorities is straightforward. For example, if tackling burglaries is a priority, the purpose of any activity will be to prevent and detect burglaries. The point is, though, that a priority is not a numerical target – a target is just an arbitrary aspirational value, such as 'to detect 21% of burglaries'.

Despite this, I still hear people say, "We need targets for burglaries because targets set direction and ambition." Wrong. The clearly-articulated priority of 'tackling burglaries' sets direction and ambition. Any associated numerical target is unnecessary.

Then, there's 'targets' vs 'measures'. I often hear the phrase, "We need targets to measure performance." Wrong again. Measures measure performance. The right measures (i.e. those derived from purpose) are absolutely critical, as they enable us to understand how the system is performing and provide information that helps us make informed decisions. But they're not targets! Targets don't measure anything – they are just random numbers invented in someone's head.

Therefore, for burglaries, appropriate measures could include:

- The burglary rate.
- Detected burglaries.
- Response times to burglaries.
- Factors that led to burglaries being detected (e.g. forensics/caught in the act/CCTV/house-to-house enquiries).

The point is that effective performance management systems require priorities and measures, but not numerical targets. The main problems with targets can be listed under two key areas:

1. All numerical targets are arbitrary.
2. No numerical target is immune from causing dysfunctional behaviour.

First, all numerical targets are arbitrary because there is no known scientific method for setting them. No matter how much in-depth analysis is undertaken to establish prevailing trajectories, parameters, or average rate of prior performance, the actual adjustment to produce the target is always arbitrary.

Such targets are usually contrived by taking a baseline (usually simplistically derived from the previous year's data – binary comparison alert!), then choosing a random number as the target. Other approaches include multiplying an arbitrary percentage against the baseline to produce the target, or 'consultation', which simply involves a group of people choosing arbitrary targets.

These approaches are fundamentally flawed, because they ignore important statistical considerations, such as – once again – the presence of normal variation. To illustrate this, see the chart below.

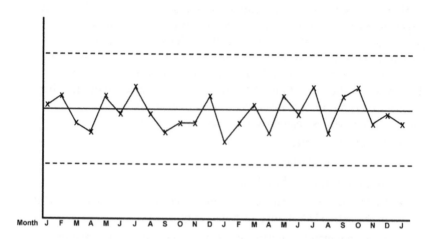

Month J F M A M J J A S O N D J F M A M J J A S O N D J

Figure 6. SPC chart displaying normal variation

Again, the axes have been left blank for simplicity, but unlike the previous SPC chart, there are no signals – therefore, it can be claimed that these data reflect a stable process where only normal variation is present. The dashed lines ('control limits') indicate the boundaries of what is normal for this process. Therefore, unless there is a change in system conditions, the data will continue to populate within this range.

Let's assume the chart relates to response times for emergencies, with the lower control limit being at the 5-minute mark and the upper control limit at 15 minutes. This means that if the type and frequency of demand remains constant, and the same resources are deployed from the same location, then officers will predictably arrive at any point within 5 and 15 minutes.

Consequently, there is no merit in setting a target (e.g. 10 minutes), because officers will continue to arrive within 5 and 15 minutes. This is because target-setting ignores variation, meaning sometimes it will be hit and other times it won't, despite constant effort. The extent of variation is determined by system conditions (such as the availability of resources, proximity to high demand locations, and so on). Similarly, if a target is set outside the expected range (e.g. at 4 minutes), then it cannot routinely be achieved under current system conditions.

Targets do not provide a method or capacity for achieving the objective of quicker response times. Altering system conditions (e.g. amount or location of resources on duty at particular times) is what influences performance; numerical targets are arbitrary and irrelevant.

Furthermore, whilst it may be possible to predict future performance within a range, it is impossible to precisely determine future performance.

For example, if the crime detection rate was steadily increasing it may be possible to predict there will be between approximately 3,000 and 3,800 offences detected in a years' time, but it would be impossible to state exactly how many (e.g. 3,450 detected offences).

Therefore, targets such as 'to detect 21% of burglaries' violate well-established statistical conventions. Such targets inadvertently suggest there is no ambition to detect the other 79% of burglaries. Surely it would be better if the ambition was to detect as many burglaries as possible – why not aim for 100% instead?

The bottom line is this – numerical targets are fundamentally incompatible with variation; there is no way round this and therefore all numerical targets are arbitrary.

The second major problem with numerical targets is that they predictably induce gaming and other dysfunctional behaviour. There is a vast range of evidence that this occurs, with plenty of examples from policing, healthcare and education.[15] For example, in policing, the Public Administration Select Committee's 2014 inquiry into misreporting of crime statistics by police forces found targets, "…tend to affect attitudes, erode data quality and to distort individual and institutional behaviour and priorities". (p.31)[16]

A further independent inquiry in 2015 confirmed strong links between the use of targets in policing and undesirable behaviour, such as pressure not to record crime, 'cherry picking' which incidents to attend, unnecessary arrests, adverse impact on morale and professional discretion, and a mindless focus on quantity over quality.[17]

These outcomes are entirely predictable, as numerical targets consistently trigger unhealthy internalised competition, resulting in a debilitating condition known as sub-optimisation. This is where individuals, teams or departments focus on targets at the expense of other important activities not subject to targets, resulting in a situation where the primary objective becomes to out-do one's peers, even at the expense of the overall system and/or the service user. Or to put it another way, targets do indeed set direction – in the direction of the targets.

Despite the evidence, some people still insist dysfunction isn't actually due to the targets, but the way they're implemented. I disagree. "If managers use targets in a particularly aggressive or punitive fashion, it stands to reason that unintended consequences are likely to be more extreme, but simply suggesting the manner in which targets are applied is the only factor in explaining behavioural dysfunction is like saying… "It's not the nails that caused the tyre to go flat – it's the way the nails were inserted into it". (Or they were the 'wrong sort' of nails, or there were 'too many'/'too few' nails, etc.) Err, no – it was the nails.

There's something innately toxic about numerical targets themselves that significantly raises the likelihood of dysfunction. During the psychometric testing element of my ongoing PhD research, I found that the use of numerical targets consistently led to adverse behavioural responses. As these experiments occurred without the additional pressure of aggressive enforcement or improper application by managers, this strongly indicates that numerical targets themselves are at least partially responsible for observed dysfunction.

An Alternative to Numerical Targets

Just don't use them.

Conclusion

So there you have it – my heresy. For years in policing and beyond, we've used the wrong type of performance information in the wrong way. We've introduced perverse incentives that cause good people to do the wrong things. I believe this situation has persisted because 'it's what we've always done' and many people are uncertain about the alternatives.

However, the alternatives are simple and free and can be implemented now by leaders at all levels; abandon the use of binary comparisons, league tables and numerical targets, then use contextualised performance information instead. Be clear about purpose, so you can set meaningful priorities, then use the right measures in the right way to understand the system, inform decision making, learn and improve.
What's not to like about that?

Simon Guilfoyle is a serving police officer, university lecturer and author

References

1 See, for example:

De Maillard, J. and Savage, S. (2012) 'Comparing Performance: The Development of Police Performance Management in France and Britain'. *Policing and Society: An International Journal of Research and Policy.* 22 (4): 363-383

Hood, C. (2007) 'Public Service Management by Numbers: Why Does it Vary? Where Has it Come From? What are the Gaps and the Puzzles?' *Public Money & Management,* 27 (2): 95-102

Loveday, B. (2005) 'The Challenge of Police Reform in England and Wales'. *Public Money and Management,* 25(5): 275–281

Pollitt, C. (2006) 'Performance Management in Practice: A Comparative Study of Executive Agencies'. *Journal of Public Administration Research and Theory,* 16 (1): 25–44

2 Home Office (2015) 'The Use of Targets in Policing'. [Online] https://www.gov.uk/government/uploads/system/uploads/attachment_data/file/466058/Review_Targets_2015.pdf [Accessed 3rd January 2016]

3 Greater London Authority (2014) London Data Store. Dashboard Theme: Crime. [Online] http://data.london.gov.uk/dashboard-summary/crime/ [Accessed 6th December 2014]

4 Bird, S. M., Cox, D., Farewell, V. T., Goldstein, H., Holt, T. and Smith, P. C. (2005) 'Performance Indicators: Good, Bad and Ugly'. *Journal of the Royal Statistical Society (A)*. 168 (1): 1-27

5 This diagram, and the subsequent SPC chart at Figure 2 are taken from: Guilfoyle, S. J. (2013) *Intelligent Policing: How Systems Thinking Methods Eclipse Conventional Management Practice*. Axminster: Triarchy Press

6 Research ongoing at time of this chapter's publication; Warwick Business School, University of Warwick.

7 Guilfoyle, S. J. (2015) 'Binary Comparisons and Police Performance Measurement: Good or Bad?' *Policing: A Journal of Policy and Practice*, 9 (2): 195-209

8 For more on SPC charts and their construction, see:

Shewhart, W. A. (1939) *Statistical Method from the Viewpoint of Quality Control*. Washington DC: The Graduate School, US Department of Agriculture

Joiner, B. (1994) *Fourth Generation Management*. McGraw-Hill

Wheeler, D.J. (2000) *Understanding Variation: The Key to Managing Chaos*. (2nd Ed.) Knoxville: SPC Press

Nielsen, M. (2015) Statistical Process Control: What is SPC? [Online] http://www.statisticalprocesscontrol.info/whatisspc.html [Accessed 30th May 2015]

9 Guilfoyle, S. J. (2015) 'Getting Police Performance Measurement under Control'. *Policing: A Journal of Policy and Practice*. doi:10.1093/police/pav027

10 See: Field, A. (2013) Discovering Statistics using IBM SPSS Statistics. London: Sage

11 See:

Goldstein, H. and Spiegelhalter, D. (1996) 'League Tables and Their Limitations: Statistical Issues in Comparisons of Institutional Performance.' *Journal of the Royal Statistical Society* 159 (3): 385-443

Bird, S. M., Cox, D., Farewell, V. T., Goldstein, H., Holt, T. and Smith, P. C. (2005) 'Performance Indicators: Good, Bad and Ugly'. *Journal of the Royal Statistical Society (A)*. 168 (1): 1-27

Jacobs, R. and Goddard, M. (2007) 'How Do Performance Indicators Add Up? An Examination of Composite Indicators in Public Services.' *Public Money & Management*, 27 (2): 103-110

12 See, for example:

Rothstein, R. (2008) 'Holding Accountability to Account'. National Center on Performance Incentives. Working Paper 2008 – 04. Nashville: Vanderbilt

Bevan, G. and Hamblin, R. (2009). 'Hitting and Missing Targets by Ambulance Services for Emergency Calls: Effects of Different Systems of Performance Measurement within the UK'. *Journal of the Royal Statistical Society* (A). 172 (1): 161 – 190

Jackson, P. M. (2011) 'Governance by Numbers: What Have We Learned Over The Past 30 Years?' *Public Money and Management*, 31 (1): 13-26

13 Guilfoyle, S. J. (2012) 'On Target? Public Sector Performance Management: Recurrent Themes, Consequences and Questions'. *Policing: A Journal of Policy and Practice*. 6 (3): 250 - 260

14 InspGuilfoyle blog – http://www.inspguilfoyle.wordpress.com

15 In addition to the papers listed at end notes 11 and 12, see also:

Bevan, G. and Hood, C. (2006) 'What's Measured is What Matters: Targets and Gaming in the English Public Healthcare System', *Public Administration*, 84 (3): 517-538

Hood, C. (2006) 'Gaming in Targetworld: The Targets Approach to Managing British Public Services'. *Public Administration Review*, 66 (4): 515-521

Seddon, J. (2008) *Systems Thinking in the Public Sector*. Axminster: Triarchy Press

Ordonez, L., Schweitzer, M., Galinsky, A. and Bazerman, M. (2009) 'Goals Gone Wild: The Systematic Side Effects of Overprescribing Goal Setting'. *Academy of Management Perspectives*. 23 (1): 6-16

Guilfoyle, S. J. (2013) *Intelligent Policing: How Systems Thinking Methods Eclipse Conventional Management Practice*. Axminster: Triarchy Press

Shorrock, S. and Licu, T. (2013) 'Target Culture: Lessons in Unintended Consequences'. *Hindsight*, No 17, Summer 2013: 10 - 16

16 PASC (House of Commons Public Administration Select Committee) (2014) 'Caught Red-Handed: Why We Can't Count on Police Recorded Crime Statistics'. [Online] http://www.publications.parliament.uk/pa/cm201314/cmselect/cmpubadm/760/760.pdf [Accessed 3rd December 2015]

17 Home Office (2015) 'The Use of Targets in Policing'. [Online] https://www.gov.uk/government/uploads/system/uploads/attachment_data/file/466058/Review_Targets_2015.pdf [Accessed 3rd January 2016]

About the Publisher

Triarchy Press is an independent publisher of alternative thinking (altThink) about government, organisations and society at large – as well as the people who participate in them.

Other titles about the application of The Vanguard Method in practice include:

The Whitehall Effect – John Seddon

Systems Thinking in the Public Sector – John Seddon

Delivering Public Services that Work (Volume 1). Systems Thinking in the Public Sector Case Studies – Peter Middleton, John Seddon

Delivering Public Services that Work (Volume 2). The Vanguard Method in the Public Sector: Case Studies – Charlotte Pell, John Seddon

Other Triarchy Press titles on organisations, leadership, systems thinking and the public sector include:

Managers as Designers in the Public Sectore – David Wastell

Ackoff's F/Laws: The Cake – Russ Ackoff

Growing Wings on the Way: Systems Thinking for Messy Situations – Rosalind Armson

Humanising Healthcare – Margaret Hannah

Intelligent Policing – Simon Guilfoyle

Managers as Designers in the Public Services – David Wastell

Systems Thinking for Curious Managers – Russ Ackoff *et al.*

The Search for Leadership: An Organisational Perspective – William Tate

Details of all these titles and others are at:

www.triarchypress.net

Lightning Source UK Ltd.
Milton Keynes UK
UKHW02f0606130218
317764UK00005B/54/P